? ARE YOU NORMAL

DAVID COX & PETER COWLING

IN CONJUNCTION WITH GALLUP POLL

ACKNOWLEDGEMENTS

Acknowledgements are due to the following organisations for their co-operation in the production of this book.

The Daily Telegraph. London Weekend Television. American Express. Flour Advisory Bureau. National Food Survey. Social Trends. Sun Life. TVS. Legal and General. Geest. Rosehaugh. Texaco.

98 Highgate West Hill,
London N6 6NR
Tel: 01 340 4399
Fax: 01 340 5413

ISBN 0 9514869-0-X

Printed in Great Britain by The Tower Press, 172 Blackstock Road, Highbury, London N5.

Distributed by Vine House Distribution, Waldenbury, North Common, Chailey, East Sussex BN8 4DR Tel: 082572 3398

? ARE YOU NORMAL - THE AUTHORS

David Cox and Peter Cowling are experienced marketeers, publishers and publicists. Working with Gallup Poll they have produced numerous research-based reports for leading commercial organisations over a number of years.

Are You Normal? is the first book in a new series that provides the reader with an insight into the average Briton's lifestyle, fears, hopes and patterns of behaviour.

For dedication beyond the realms of normality, the authors would like to thank Jilly, Paula, Gail, Susan and Laurence.

? ARE YOU NORMAL

INTRODUCTION

Is it normal to believe in ghosts? Go on holiday to Greece? Talk to your pet goldfish?

Are you normal in thinking that Prince Charles will never be King? Or that making love is the most popular thing to do in bed?

These are but a few of the dozens of issues and questions on British behaviour that come under the microscope in this book.

Over 60,000 adults have been interviewed to produce a comprehensive and fascinating snapshot of the British at work, rest and play.

For many years Gallup Poll has used well-established techniques of measurement in order to chart what the British think about a wide range of issues. This book explains those techniques and goes on to identify what is average and therefore normal.

In parts it is serious. In others, it's fun. Whoever you are and wherever you are, it is a book that will provide the answer to so many of those questions that you never dared to ask.

FOREWORD

Here is your chance to see how far your attitudes, opinions and behaviour match those of the general public. You can also see how good you are in knowing what the public thinks.

How has this book come about? Every week Gallup interviewers are out on the streets knocking on doors asking thousands of people a wide range of questions. The responses to hundreds of thousands of such interviews have gone into this book.

How are polls conducted? And how can they be representative when only 1000 or 2000 people are interviewed?

Let us assume we want to interview 1000 people. First 100 cities, towns and villages are selected based on Government population statistics. These places are spread across the country to cover England, Scotland and Wales, and range from rural areas to inner cities.

Each interviewer, using a variety of methods, finds a good mix of ten adults at each location, taking into account their sex, age and class. Collectively, these 1,000 people represent a national sample of the adult population. It is a base that can be checked against known Government statistics.

Can 1000 or so from a total of more than 40 million be representative?

Accurate representation is not really a function of size. A sample of 100 people, interviewed following the above lines, could be just as representative as a sample of 1000, ten times as many, though the larger sample would be more accurate - if both were representative.

Think of a stew when you want to know whether it contains enough salt. You stir it and then taste a spoonful. From that small amount you decide either to add more salt or not. You have assumed, by the very act of stirring and sampling, that the spoonful tastes the same as the rest of the stew. This is exactly what pollsters set out to do.

Why have I never been interviewed, you may ask. The odds are roughly evens that you have been. As of the middle of 1988, nearly one in two said they had been interviewed (before Gallup got to them).

Out of interest, a slightly lower figure was obtained in France a few months earlier.

With a population of more than 40 million adults, continually growing and changing, it is hardly surprising that not everybody has been interviewed. But hold on, we'll get around to you!

Bob Wybrow
Director
Gallup Poll

Note: In some cases the figures in the tables do not add up to 100. Where this occurs it is because respondents have stated more than one preference.

? ARE YOU NORMAL

CONTENTS

? ARE YOU NORMAL

PRODUCTS BY POST

T-Shirts and Greetings cards can also be ordered by post.

Simply fill in the form at the back of this book.

Pay by Access/Mastercard or Visa card or send a cheque or postal order.

GENERAL

Royalty

God

Christmas

Ghosts

Weather

ROYALTY

Who is the most popular member of the Royal family?

The elegant Princess Diana with that shy smile and love of glitzy fashion? The warm and charming Queen Mother? Or the outspoken, horse-loving champion of children in need, Princess Anne?

Wrong. The British say Charles, their next King, is top of the Royal pops with a fifth of the nation voting for him.

The nation's favourite Grandma, The Queen Mother, is our second choice, with Princess Di and Princess Anne sharing third place honours.

They both narrowly beat The Queen who polled an eighth of the nation's vote. Prince Philip and Princess Margaret won a few votes to emerge near the bottom of the list. Prince Andrew also managed to scrape in, but no votes are recorded for Prince Edward.

More men than women voted for Prince Charles but one in eight of us have doubts as to whether he will ever become King.

What should he do instead?

Become an architect say most of us, given his frequent criticisms of modern buildings it would seem a suitable conclusion. However, there are many who have other ideas. Try diplomacy say 21 per cent. What next? Intriguingly, suitability as a social worker narrowly beats a farmer into fourth place. Lowest on the potential work roster came doctor, lawyer, priest and licensee.

Our fascination with Royalty and news of their exploits remains insatiable. Witness the dozens of magazines, books and videos on the subject. But how many of us are ever likely to get any closer than a glimpse of the Royal Coach? And what would you do if you were informed that our Monarch intends to drop by for tea?

Over the half the country thought the proposition so unlikely they didn't even answer.

A quarter would mow the lawn and a tenth would buy new cups and saucers.

One in 20 would buy a new lavatory seat cover just in case. And one in ten would grab a brush and repaint the house. Twice as many women as men would find the occasion a perfect excuse to buy new clothes!

What would you do?

Now the ticklish question of the Royal "we". Do you think the Prime Minister should listen more to the Queen when formulating policy? Listen less or leave things as they are?

Listen more to Her Majesty say over half the nation, with a third recommending that the current relationship remains as it is.

WHO IS YOUR FAVOURITE MEMBER OF THE ROYAL FAMILY?

	%
Prince Charles	21
Queen Mother	14
Princess Anne	13
Princess Diana	13
The Queen	12
Duchess of York	3
Prince Andrew	2
Princess Margaret	1
Prince Philip	1
Prince Edward	0
Other	20

IF PRINCE CHARLES HAD TO GET A JOB, WHICH, IF ANY, OF THESE DO YOU THINK HE WOULD BE BEST SUITED TO DO?

	%
Architect	29
Diplomat	21
Social worker	12
Farmer	11
Politician	9
None of these	7
Teacher	4
Lawyer	3
Doctor	1
Engineer	1
Publican	1
Priest	1

GOD

Do you believe in God? The Devil? Heaven? Hell?

The Devil fares very badly with the British, only a fifth say he exists. Hell also gets low marks.

God on the other hand is a much better proposition, with over two thirds of the nation believing in His or Her existence.

And half of British adults believe in Heaven.

Do you believe that Jesus Christ was the Son of God or just a man. Half of people believe he was the Son of God, with a third saying that he was just a man. One in 12 believe it is just a story.

Belief in God does not necessarily mean you are religious. This is especially highlighted among young adults. In the 16 to 24 year old group, four out of five said they believe in God.

Yet only five per cent claim to be very religious, with almost a third saying they were somewhat religious. Two thirds of young people said they are not religious at all.

If there is a God, is he a personal God, or do we believe more in some sort of spirit or life force? At least four in ten go for the idea of a spirit with three in ten believing in a personal God.

One in four Britons are atheists. While half of us never go to church or almost never go to church, a quarter may pop in a few times a year. One in eight is a regular churchgoer, making a visit every week or more.

Our religious beliefs are complex, with two thirds stating that the Bible is essential to the Christian Church, and just under a third say the church will still survive even if the idea that the Bible is of divine authority were to be rejected.

Nearly half think the Old Testament is a collection of stories and fables. Slightly fewer people believe this of the New Testament.

If you have ever been aware of a kindly presence looking after you or guiding you then you are not alone. One in five agree it is more than likely to happen.

Some people go even further. One in six say they have been aware of a secret presence in nature. A quarter have been aware of God.

Does praying help you with problems? Three-quarters declare that they have never been aware of receiving help in answer to a prayer.

Only one in ten has been aware of being in an evil presence. For some strange reason this nasty feeling is four times as likely to happen among the rich rather than the poor.

The richer you are, the less likely you are to believe in Heaven.

WHICH, IF ANY, OF THE FOLLOWING DO YOU BELIEVE IN?

THE DEVIL?	%
Yes	21
No	74
Don't know	5
HELL?	
Yes	21
No	73
Don't know	6
HEAVEN?	
Yes	52
No	42
Don't know	6
GOD?	
Yes	68
No	26
Don't know	6
REINCARNATION?	
Yes	25
No	62
Don't know	13

HAVE YOU FELT AN AWARENESS OF THE PRESENCE OF GOD?

	%
Never	73
Once or twice	6
Several times	9
Constantly	12

CHRISTMAS

What do we all do on the great festive occasion, Christmas?

Three quarters of the nation like staying at home to enjoy a turkey and watch the lights twinkle on the tree.

Not surprisingly, it's the 35 to 44 year olds with children who are even more committed with well over 80 per cent preferring the comforts of home to visits to the seaside or country.

One in two of us will have a family party and one in ten will head for the local pantomime.

But is Christmas a religious festival or a holiday? An opportunity to meet the family and friends? Or just an occasion for eating and drinking?

There is a wide divergence of opinion depending on how old you are. The younger you are, the less likely you are to believe it is primarily religious, placing greater emphasis on eating, drinking and meeting friends. However, half the nation's senior citizens regard Christmas mainly as a religious festival.

Do we think Christmas is becoming more or less religious than when we were children?

Three quarters say definitely less religious, with the elderly even more firmly committed to the notion.

This overall view is echoed by the church attendance figures on Christmas Day. Almost three quarters say they normally do not go to church on Christmas Day.

Back at home, almost half the men are to be found stuffing the turkey and a third of the Great British public claim to enjoy the task!

Is a turkey normal for the festive feast? Yes say most of us. When does the normal family eat? Three quarters of the nation are to be found clutching their cutlery between noon and 3pm, while another fifth attack the turkey between 3pm and 5pm. A mere four per cent will wait until after 6pm.

And if you want to continue to conform on Christmas Day, then watch the Queens' speech on television. You will be among half the nation that does so.

WHICH, IF ANY, OF THESE THINGS ARE YOU DOING AT CHRISTMAS?

	%
Having a christmas tree	79
Having a turkey or other poultry	77
Staying at home	73
Having a family party	52
Filling children's stockings	38
Going to a pantomime	11
Going away to the seaside or country	8
None of these	2

DO YOU REGARD CHRISTMAS MAINLY AS ...

	%
A religious festival	34
An opportunity to meet the family and friends	31
A holiday	23
An occasion for eating and drinking	13

WOULD YOU SAY THAT CHRISTMAS IS BECOMING MORE RELIGIOUS, LESS RELIGIOUS, OR REMAINING ABOUT THE SAME COMPARED WITH YOUR CHILDHOOD?

	%
More religious	3
Less religious	74
Same	22
Don't know	1

GHOSTS

Have you ever seen a ghost? Over one in ten British adults claim to have done so. This is not so surprising when you consider that over a quarter of the population believe in ghosts, and that a third of 18-34 year-olds hold the belief. The old folks however are rather more sceptical with less than one in five saying they believe.

But the notion of the paranormal is strong. Forty per cent believe in life after death, with over half of all women believing they will be moving on to some other role once their time on earth has ended. Men are rather less optimistic with less than one in three believing there is a new world beyond the cemetery gates.

Over half of adults believe in thought-transference between two people, with women more adamant than men that this can happen.

Black magic is given the thumbs down by most, with almost nine in ten adults saying they just don't believe in it.

Hypnotism is much more acceptable, with over a third being convinced it works - particularly the young.

Flying saucers? On average one in five believe they exist but a quarter of 18-34 year olds believe in them.

It is quite normal to believe in the powers of faith healing, as almost half the adult population say they accept the possibilities of mind over matter.

Over half of us believe it is possible to forecast that something is going to happen before it actually does. Middle-class women are above-average believers in this form of intuition.

One in five Britons believe in the power of lucky charms or mascots but three out of four say it is not possible to exchange messages with the dead.

But whether or not you believe in any of these, there is one set of circumstances that is definitely very normal.

Over 60 per cent of British adults claim to have experienced that weird phenomenon of having said or done something exactly the same on an earlier occasion.

Just in case you are wondering whether it is normal to have your fortune told, you should know that one in four have paid to hear a forecast of their future.

WEATHER

We all know it is normal to talk about the weather, but how much does it influence our lives?

When you get dressed for example, do you take into account what the weather forecasters say?

Surprisingly, almost two thirds say they do not take any notice, although women are more likely than men to do so. Certainly, the younger you are, the less you will heed the weather forecast. The wealthy are the least concerned about matching their clothes to suit the weather conditions, while the lower income groups are most likely to take notice of the sun or showers advice.

WHEN YOU GET DRESSED, DO YOU TAKE INTO ACCOUNT WHAT THE WEATHER FORECASTS HAVE SAID?

	%
Yes	35
No	61
Never watch or listen to weather forecasts	4

Larry

ROMANCE

Marriage

Bed

Sex

MARRIAGE

Are shotgun weddings out of date? They seem to be. Three out of four adults think it is no longer necessary to get married if you are single and pregnant.

But attitudes towards the issue change depending where you live and how old you are. A shotgun wedding is most likely in the North East and least likely in Scotland and Wales.

Years ago, pregnancy outside marriage was a social sin of the first order. Now, the whispering and pointing is left to the bigots.

If you are young, it will be your friends who show the least concern, particularly girls. Nine out of ten young women feel that pregnancy does not automatically mean marriage.

But you will have more of a problem explaining to your grandparents. They are going to find it much harder to understand with 44 per cent of over 65's still saying that unmarried women should not have a baby outside wedlock. You have about an even chance they will give you their blessing.

Mum and Dad are likely to be much more relaxed than their parents were. After all, they probably grew up in the swinging sixties themselves. Their generation originated the free-living, free-loving society. That is probably why the vast majority of the middle-aged say it's now acceptable to stay single even if you are going to have a baby.

Is it normal to be happily married? Yes, say almost four out of five married couples who are "very satisfied" with the relationship.

But given the rising divorce rate, surprisingly only four per cent say they are not at all satisfied.

This dissatisfaction may have something to do with money. Twice as many of the poorest couples are unhappy with each other than the richest.

Contentment is highest in the Midlands and Wales and the unhappiest couples are most likely to be found in the South.

What annoys married couples?

Nagging by the wife is the greatest annoyance for men, while the husband's untidiness is top of the list of irritations among wives.

Smoking is second on the women's list, which also annoys men. But husbands and boyfriends thought 'moods' just as annoying. Equally as bad for some men is the way their partner spends money, particularly on clothes.

Husbands who "work late" is another cause of annoyance for some women. And if these are the men that fall asleep as soon as they get home then they could well be in the women's next most annoying category - snoring.

Either women do not snore, or men couldn't care less if they do or don't, for snoring is not among the men's complaints.

Mens' selfishness, or lack of consideration, is more annoying to women than the same fault in themselves is to men. Similarly, mens' forgetfulness is more of an issue among women. "He's always forgetting things." "He says he hasn't been told things," are frequent complaints.

There are a few abnormal marriages - like the one in five who say that nothing annoys them about their partner.

Who does the housework is a major issue.

Over a third of married women claim their husbands never lift a finger to help with the housework. And another third say help from their husbands only happens occasionally.

A fifth of all British men are either very lucky, very lazy, or both. They admit that they never do any housework, never either lay or clear the table, and never cook.

The one task which men claim to do most regularly is the shopping. Over half say they shop once a week and a quarter say shopping is a daily routine.

The majority of British still think marriage is a great idea, with almost seven out of ten saying that a "good marriage" is among their top ambitions.

Does class enter into the marriage equation and just how acceptable do we think it is for a woman to marry a man from a lower social class, or vice versa?

It really isn't an issue for most people, with over four in five finding it an acceptable practice.

BED

Sleeping naked is normal for nearly half of all British men while only one in five women confesses to sleeping in the nude.

What do we wear in bed? For a woman, the nightdress is still the most popular garment and the older she is, the greater the chance of wearing one. The nightdress is followed by pyjamas and then a night shirt.

What do we do in bed apart from sleep? Making love is chosen by a fifth of the nation, as the favourite activity. Twice as many women as men select reading rather than making love in bed as their number one choice.

One in five women enjoys reading in bed most, and some gossips even admit that talking is the most enjoyable pastime once between the sheets.

Only a handful of people say watching TV in bed is their top priority. Not surprisingly, most married people sleep together in the same bed, but as couples grow older they tend to have separate beds. Among the over 65's group, a quarter sleep in separate beds and one in six sleep in separate rooms.

Women do not sleep as well as men. A bad night's sleep at least once or twice a week is normal for half of them. They wake up more often in the night and are more likely to take sleeping pills or tranquilizers.

Dreaming occurs frequently yet most of the adult population claims that they rarely or never have a nightmare.

Only a fifth of us say a prayer at bedtime with women more likely to do so.

For most of us, getting up in the morning presents the worst moment of the day. And oddly enough not many take tea in bed. Just a quarter of the nation likes to 'sup before they are up', during the week, but most wait for the weekend before enjoying a cuppa in bed.

WHAT DO YOU NORMALLY WEAR IN BED?

	MEN %	WOMEN %
SUMMER:		
Pyjama bottoms only	16	0
Pyjamas	26	3
Nightdress	0	69
Nightshirt	1	6
Other	12	2
Nothing	45	20
WINTER:		
Pyjama bottoms only	10	0
Pyjamas	40	11
Nightdress	0	70
Nightshirt	1	7
Other	11	2
Nothing	38	10

HOW OFTEN WOULD YOU SAY YOU HAVE A BAD NIGHT'S SLEEP?

	%
Most nights	13
3 or 4 nights a week	7
Once or twice a week	17
Less often	41
Never	21

HOW OFTEN WOULD YOU SAY YOU DREAM?

Most nights	28
3 or 4 nights a week	9
Once or twice a week	16
Less often	30
Never	16

HOW OFTEN WOULD YOU SAY YOU HAVE NIGHTMARES?

Most nights	1
3 or 4 nights a week	1
Once or twice a week	3
Less often	30
Never	65

HOW OFTEN WOULD YOU SAY YOU WAKE UP DURING THE NIGHT?

Most nights	35
3 or 4 nights a week	9
Once or twice a week	17
Less often	23
Never	16

SEX

While one per cent of British men claim to have experienced sexual intercourse with over 100 women, the typical male has had one sexual partner in the previous 12 months with a fifth claiming to have had sex with more than ten women, and a tenth having never made love.

How old are we when we make love for the first time? For most it happens when we are 18, although women are more likely than men to have had sexual intercourse before they are 24.

Almost half of women say they have had sex with only one man and a fifth admit to never having had sex ever. Another fifth say they have had two sexual partners and another tenth say three partners. Ten or more sexual partners are claimed by less than one in 20 women.

The use of condoms has been cited as a way of avoiding the likelihood of contracting the virus that leads to the killer AIDS. So how widely should condoms be made available?

Should condom machines be available for example in schools attended by 11-15 year olds? No say four in five adults. But they change their minds once the pupils are 16 or over. Then such machines should be made available say almost half the parents.

HOW MANY HETEROSEXUAL PARTNERS HAVE YOU HAD IN YOUR LIFETIME?

	WOMEN %	MEN %
None	5	9
One	46	29
Two	18	12
Three	11	8
Four	7	7
Five	4	5
Six	3	3
Seven	1	2
Eight	1	2
Nine	0	1
Ten or more	4	22

HAVE YOU EVER EXPERIENCED 'LOVE AT FIRST SIGHT'?

	%
Yes	35
No	65

THE USE OF PORNOGRAPHY CAN HELP SOME MARRIAGES?

	%
Strongly agree	1
Agree	29
Neither	12
Disagree	28
Strongly disagree	11
Don't know	19

RECENTLY SOME LOCAL EDUCATIONAL AUTHORITIES HAVE SUGGESTED INSTALLING MACHINES SELLING CONTRACEPTIVES (CONDOMS) IN SCHOOLS. DO YOU APPROVE OR DISAPPROVE OF INSTALLING SUCH MACHINES WHERE THEY CAN BE USED BY:

	%
11-15 year olds	
Approve	15
Disapprove	81
Don't know	4
16 year olds	
Approve	44
Disapprove	52
Don't know	5
17 year olds or older	
Approve	55
Disapprove	40
Don't know	5

GENERALLY SPEAKING, DO YOU PREFER WOMEN WHO ARE ...

	%
Older than you	13
Younger than you	14
About the same age	58
No preference	15

DO YOU GENERALLY PREFER ...

	%
Blondes	29
Brunettes	28
Red Heads	3
No preference	40

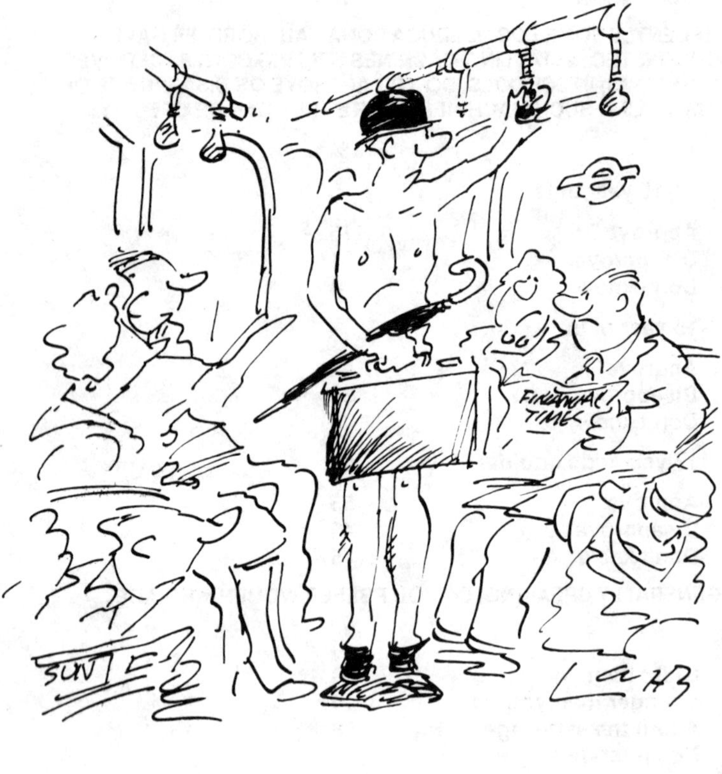
FINANCIAL TIMES
SUN
LARRY

FINANCE

Money

Insurance

Work

Honesty

Cars

MONEY

The accumulation of money, or lack of it, provides endless debates - is it normal to be rich or poor?

Most of us slot into the boring bit of being neither one nor the other. But for sheer vicarious pleasure, one in three of us claim to have met a millionaire, with people in the North East claiming a higher than average acquaintance with this fast growing breed.

Do we all have the same chance of becoming rich provided we have the energy and talent?

No, say the majority. Only a quarter of the nation subscribes to the view. But almost three quarters of us believe that becoming rich depends upon our parentage. In fact, two thirds believe that social class is a crucial element in the determination to become rich.

And a third of us believe inheritance is the principal reason that someone becomes rich. Hard work is the second requirement and exceptional ability comes third.

Who do we think are the richest people in Britain? Large landowners such as the monarchy and titled people spill to the surface.. They are closely followed by popular entertainers. So if your daddy doesn't own a few million acres of moorland yet still the pound notes beckon, then a career in front of the cameras might be on the cards. Indeed, showbiz is seen as the easiest way to get rich quick.

Would you be happier if you were rich?

Almost half of us think not, with equal quarters believing they would either be far happier or less happy.

But beware if you are intent on becoming rich, because half of us believe that rich people's lives are more stressful.

They may be better educated, more ruthless, ambitious, greedy, power-hungry and snobbish than most but in the nation's view the wealthy are marginally less generous, hard-working and sympathetic.

What is your assessment of how the rich get rich? By fair means or foul? If you heard of someone who started with almost nothing and had become very rich, do you think it is likely that they had achieved their wealth while being honest all the time; or that they probably have something to hide?

The average person thinks that only a quarter of the rich have obtained their money honestly.

Self-made wealth is more greatly admired than inherited wealth.

The self-made rich deserve their wealth say four out of five. They are admired by 78 per cent of the population and almost half believe they do a good job for the nation. People who inherit wealth however, are viewed by half of us as lazy, and one in six see these rich people as a burden on society.

But making a lot of money is not as important to us as we might think. Whilst it is fine for a third, two thirds think the opposite. Having said that, almost two thirds of us would like to be free of financial worries, and a sixth would like to be sufficiently well-off to have plenty of spare money in the bank.

How do you view your chances of becoming rich? Pretty remotely say the majority - 82 per cent think it fairly or not at all likely, while only one in six think it is an achievable goal.

Over half of us would be prepared to work a lot harder if it were to make us significantly better off, but few are prepared to sacrifice time with family and friends and give up leisure time in order to coin in the cash. Neither is the normal person prepared to take risks to get rich. Over nine in ten say they are not prepared to gamble their savings or give up a secure job.

Freedom from money worries is given as the main reason why a normal member of the public would like to become rich.

Do we believe the rich make a crucial contribution to the British economy because they invest their money to create jobs and prosperity? Definitely not, say three quarters. In fact, most Britons believe quite the reverse. The majority view is that the rich put their money where they can make the quickest profit, be it in Britain or abroad and certainly don't put Britain and the British jobs first.

What about handing over your wealth to your family when you have finally made it? Almost nine out of ten agree that a person should have the right to hand on wealth to his or her children.

Who do we think deserves to be rich? People who start their own businesses say 87 per cent, putting them at the top of the deserving league table.

Popular entertainers are singled out by 55 per cent of the nation, and politicians are hot on their trail, with 46 per cent of our vote.

The majority of people (87 per cent) believe that nurses are the worst paid members of the working community with teachers (39 per cent) coming next in line for sympathy.

How much money should any one individual be allowed to have is an interesting question, and should there be a ceiling?

A third of us say the amount of wealth should be pegged and half of those in favour of such a move believe that the ceiling should be no more than £1 million.

Similarly, a third believe that salaries should be limited and two thirds of this group say keep the annual earnings under £100,000.

Have you ever been left any money in a will? Twenty eight per cent of Britons have. Not surprisingly, the chances of a windfall rise the richer or older you are, with 40 per cent of pensioners claiming to have benefitted.

On average how much are people left? For most beneficiaries (46 per cent) it's a token £500 or less. but a fifth pocket between £2,000-£10,000.

If you totted up all that you own with the exception of your home, what do you reckon you would be worth?

A fifth of the nation say even if they sold everything they would still owe money.

A third of us, having sold up, would be left with anything from £1,000-£10,000. Another fifth estimate up to £50,000 with only one per cent of us being worth over £150,000.

PEOPLE VISUALISE BEING RICH IN DIFFERENT WAYS. WHAT FOR YOU IS THE MOST IMPORTANT THINGS THAT BEING RICH WOULD BRING?

	%
Freedom from worry about money	59
Having a luxurious lifestyle	12
A large sum of money in bank or in stocks or shares	7
Owning property - say land or houses	7
A high annual salary	4
Not having to work	4
Other benefits	3
Power over the lives of other people	2
Don't know/No answer	2

HAVE YOU EVER MET A MILLIONAIRE?

	%
No	48
Yes	47
Don't know/No answer	5

INSURANCE

What does the average Briton think about insurance? It depends on what is being insured. Only a quarter for example are covered by a health insurance scheme that provides payment for private medical treatment.

Among the over 65's - the sector of society most likely to need medical treatment, disregard for this type of insurance rises to 83 per cent.

On the other hand, 95 per cent of householders do have a house contents insurance policy.

How often do we make a claim for loss or damage? A third have made a claim in the past five years with the most frequent claims being for accidental damage (13 per cent) plumbing or flooding (10 per cent) burglary (6 per cent) and fire (5 per cent).

If you have made a claim then the chances are you were satisfied with the way the insurance company dealt with it - a view held by 83 per cent - and you thought the amount awarded was right.

But how honest are we about making insurance claims? Age is significant. Most people think that the over 50's are half as likely than average to claim more than the value of their loss. While 18-24 year olds are perceived to be the group most likely to take advantage of the insurance company and exaggerate the size of the loss and claim.

FOR WHICH INSURANCE SITUATIONS HAVE YOU CLAIMED, IF ANY, OVER THE PAST FIVE YEARS?

	%
Accidental damage	13
Plumbing/Flood	10
Burglary	6
Fire damage	5
Article/Money stolen	3
Storm/Gale damage	2
Other	1
Never claimed	65

WORK

Hard work is back in fashion.

Even the Royal family's performance of official functions comes under the media spotlight.

But is it natural to like work and are we in danger of becoming a nation of workaholics?

If you are satisfied with the work you do then you are normal. Almost two-thirds of the working population say they like their job, with men enjoying work more than women.

The upper and middle classes like their job more than most, while lower income groups are the least satisfied with their daily toil.

What time does the average Briton wake up and get to work?

Four in five are out of the house by 7.30am.

An alarm is necessary to wake four in ten workers, while as many again wake up automatically in time for work.

How long does it take to shake off the slumbers and leave for work?

For one in 25, it is a mere 15 minutes between lifting the head from the pillow and starting out for the factory or office. A fifth are on their way within half an hour, while four in ten need at least an hour.

Half the nation travels to work by car, a fifth by public transport, 16 per cent by walking and six per cent by bicycle.

What is normal when we get to work? Over half stand all day to complete their job, with Southerners far more likely than Northerners being able to sit. Do we enjoy work? A quarter say they must do because time passes so quickly, and for most people, the working day passes reasonably quickly.

But for another quarter, time drags and among this group of clock watchers, three per cent say that time almost stands still.

What might make us work harder?

Fear of unemployment is a main motivator for two-thirds of the nation, especially those with a mortgage, but nine out of ten say a share of the profits would induce them to put in a bit more effort.

Over half the workforce say they would prefer shares in their company to a pay increase of the same value, with 85 per cent agreeing that this course of action would improve the country's economy.

Are you ever late for work? Two thirds say they never are. One in four are late occasionally, but a small minority admit to being late every day.

If you are well-off, young, or live in the Midlands or Wales then you are likely to be among the worst timekeepers.

What do you wear at work? A third of men change into special clothes when they arrive at work, and for 43 per cent a tie is considered obligatory!

Who is prepared to say they have never ever taken advantage of their employer? Not many. Men sneak more company-time than women and are twice as likely to read at work and four times more likely to do the crossword than women.

Two in five workers admit to using the firm's phone to make personal calls and one in ten write personal letters in company time.

Does the average worker think he or she is paid enough? Half of us think we are underpaid and a quarter believe they are substantially underpaid.

Young, single workers feel they get the rawest pay deal, while the further north you live, the greater the satisfaction with the paypacket.

What about working women?

Four in five men said mothers should be able to work full-time. Men and women in each age group were in general agreement with each other.

More disagreement came between the young and the elderly, particularly between grandfathers and their granddaughters. Over eight in ten young women under 25 do not feel their place is in the home, yet half the men over 65 thought they were wrong.

Women with young children working full-time are however, still frowned upon by more than half the nation. Greatest disapproval came from grannies. Three-quarters of women over 65 declaring that women with children under five years should not work.

If it is becoming normal for women with children to work, what should be done to help them?

Training after having children is the top priority say four in five. Nursery care, play groups and guaranteed re-employment for young mothers are called for by three-quarters, while tax relief for women who pay for a child minder is also specified.

WOULD YOU SAY THAT FOR THE WORK YOU DO, YOU ARE OR ARE NOT PAID ENOUGH

	%
Paid enough	46
Not paid enough - a lot	23
Not paid enough - a little	22
Not paid enough - not sure	4
Don't know whether pay is enough or not	2
Don't know	3

IF YOU HAD THE CHANCE, WOULD YOU LIKE TO DO A COMPLETELY DIFFERENT JOB?

	%
Yes	45
Depends	9
No	44
Don't know	2

HOW INTERESTED WOULD YOU SAY THE WORK YOU DO WAS:

	%
Very interesting	39
Fairly interesting	41
Fairly boring	11
Very boring	7
Don't know	2

DO YOU THINK TWO WORKING PARTNERS CREATE MORE STRESS OR LESS STRESS IN A MARRIAGE?

	%
More stress	38
Less stress	27
No difference	22
Don't know	13

IF THE WOMAN OF THE HOUSE COULD EARN ENOUGH TO BE THE SOLE WAGE EARNER, WOULD YOU APPROVE OR DISAPPROVE OF THE HUSBAND STAYING AT HOME TO TAKE CARE OF THE HOUSE AND FAMILY

	%
Approve	61
Disapprove	33
Don't know	6

HONESTY

How honest is the average Briton? It all depends on how old you are and the potential crime involved. Failing to hand in an umbrella you have found to a Lost Property Office is one thing, but stealing from a supermarket, or buying a cheap video recorder you think has been stolen, is something quite different.

A third of the nation think that not paying the bus-fare if a conductor forgets to ask is very dishonest unless you happen to be 18-34. Only a quarter of this group believe fare dodging is very dishonest, compared with half the over 50's.

And how dishonest is it not telling a shop-assistant that you have been given too much change? Once again, a third say it is a very dishonest action, but the young are not so sure with only a fifth saying it's very dishonest.

What about the taxman? How dishonest is, for example, not declaring all that you should? Four out of ten agree it is very dishonest behaviour.

Gazumping someone in a house sale is viewed as an extremely dishonest action among over half the nation, but overclaiming on an insurance policy is not perceived as quite such a bad crime.

Who do we think are the most honest members of society? Doctors and the clergy win the highest rating, while journalists, builders, salesmen, estate agents and advertising executives were reckoned to have the lowest ethical and honesty standards.

WHICH OF THE FOLLOWING DO YOU THINK ARE VERY DISHONEST?

Not paying your fare on the bus if the conductor forgets to ask	
Very dishonest	**35%**
Not telling a shop assistant that you've been given too much change	
Very dishonest	**36%**
Not declaring all that you should to the Tax man	
Very dishonest	**42%**
Not reporting that the building society has paid too much money into your account	
Very dishonest	**65%**
Not reporting that you've found a purse with £10 in	
Very dishonest	**65%**
Stealing an item from a large supermarket	
Very dishonest	**91%**

CARS

For the average Briton owning a car comes second after a home in a list of investment priorities.

So it's quite normal to want a car, but what sort of car? A reliable runner that's economical? Or a fast-lane job with all the trimmings?

Judging from the attention advertising copywriters give to performance, it's m.p.h. rather thatn m.p.g. that takes the nation's fancy. Fantasy plays a big part. So too does fashion. Once Grand Prix spectators saw the spoilers on their racing heroes' machines, it wasn't long before appendages looking like giant picnic trays, started appearing on the back of family cars.

So what should you aim to buy in order to have the most fashionable wheels? A Porsche.

According to Gallup's Poll of what is in and out of fashion, Porsche's are claimed to be "In" by over two thirds. But hot on their wheels, is Ford with just under two thirds of the nation believing that this is the car to drive.

Other trendy vehicles? Four in ten of the nation votes the classic Volkswagen Beetle in - despite the fact that it is out of production. Ferraris are apparently not so fashionable. A third (38 per cent) of adults vote them "In", as opposed to 35 per cent who say they're "Out".

How normal is it to own a a driving licence? Over four in ten say they have one and a third claim to have passed their driving test first time!

Almost one in five gained a licence after two attempts, with almost one in ten being awarded the coveted prize at their third try.

Where are you most likely to pass your driving test first time? For anxious would-be drivers, go West - four out of ten passed first time in the South West. But avoid Wales, only a quarter passed their test on their first outing with the driving inspector.

Oddly enough, rural areas such as East Anglia and the South West have fewer than average licence holders - perhaps the age of the horse has yet to be overtaken?

If you think drivers who drink alcohol before driving should lose their licence, then you are not alone. This view is held by half the nation.

Drinking and driving has become an important issue and one where the average member of the public would like more stringent regulations imposed.

When asked whether alcohol limits allowed under the present law are strict enough, 60 per cent say they are not. Have you ever driven after drinking alcohol? Almost one in three of us say we have. If you happen to be well-off, then the greater the chances that you have, with over 40 per cent getting behind the wheel after a snifter or two.

Four in ten drivers, who have been drinking, say they are not deterred by being breathalysed.

And in spite of the clampdown, a quarter of the nation's drivers admit to having driven when they thought they had drunk too much alcohol to drive safely.

What are the chances of being breathalysed? Only one in ten drivers has been invited to blow in the bag.

What is the likelihood of you or someone else in your home running a car? Over 70 per cent of households have at least one car and a fifth own two or more.

Where you live and what you earn are crucial to how many cars you own. A quarter of Southerners fit in the multi-wheels bracket, while the Scots are least likely to own two cars or more.

What is the average estimated value of your car? Seven out of ten of car owners estimate £7,000 or below. Only two per cent reckon over £15,000 unless you happen to be in the most affluent sector of society in which case the level rises to reach seven per cent.

What about servicing? What does it cost and do we believe the moving parts ever really get oiled when the garage greasers go to work?

One in seven of us suspect that the lubrication and service checklist is never completed properly in spite of spending on average over £100 per service.

Does the average driver find anything else to complain about car servicing? Yes, cost, say a quarter. With another one in seven doubting the competence of the service staff!

LEISURE

Gardening

Sport

Eating

Drinking

Restaurants

Clothes

GARDENING

Rose Cottage is the most popular house name in Britain, so perhaps it is not so surprising to discover that our favourite flower is also...the rose.

As the national emblem for England, it's natural to expect it to climb to the top of the list as the most loved flower. In Scotland and Wales its colour and scent are just as much appreciated as in the gardens of Kent. A third of all Britons choose the rose as their favourite flower to grow. And the older you are then the more appealing its fragrance becomes.

The daffodil brightens up many lives in Spring and is the second favourite British bloom. And in the hills and valleys of Wales it is more popular than in any other part of the British Isles. A fifth of all Welsh gardeners prefer growing golden daffodils to the sometimes thorny problem of raising roses.

When the British look for their third choice, then carnations and chrysanthemums bloom into sight.

But whoever in the family plants the seeds and weeds the edges, women are more decisive than men at choosing their favourite flowers. Nearly a third of men had no special favourite in the garden. Twice as many men as women say they don't blooming care.

Buying flowers as opposed to growing them puts the men in a more decisive mood. And perhaps a more romantic one.

Roses for their loved ones are clear favourites with men. Women place them equally alongside carnations with freesias not far behind.

If you want your man to buy you roses then you stand the best chance if he is a Geordie. In the Tyne Tees area, almost two thirds of men select the romantic rose as their best buy. But don't raise your hopes too high if you live in East Anglia. There, only a third of men shell out for roses.

Men and women agree that the dahlia is one of the least popular blooms but only fractionally behind the iris and the lily.

Buy tickets for Amsterdam if you want tulips. And if you are expecting someone to give you gladioli then book seats for the next Dame Edna show.

WHAT IS YOUR FAVOURITE FLOWER TO GROW?

	%
Roses	34
No favourite flower	23
Other	14
Daffodils	12
Carnations	5
Chrysanthemums	4
Dahlias	2
Freesias	2
Tulips	2
Gladioli	1
Lillies	1
Iris	0

WHAT IS YOUR FAVOURITE FLOWER TO BUY?

	%
Roses	31
Carnations	20
No favourite flower	14
Freesias	10
Daffodils	9
Chrysanthemums	7
Other	4
Tulips	2
Iris	1
Gladioli	1
Lillies	1

SPORT

The majority of British love sport. As long as they can watch it on television it seems. For almost six in ten of British adults admit they never participate in any form of sport.

Disinclination rises to seven in ten among women and almost nine in ten of the elderly. But not all grans and grandads give up. Almost one in ten of the nation's elder folk participate in some form of sporting activity at least once a week.

Men are far more likely than women to participate. So too are singles, the young, and the well-off.

The keenest sportsmen are in the South of whom 29 per cent participate in sport at least once a week. They are marginally ahead of Scots and Northerners with 27 per cent regularly making a sporting appearance as a player, not a spectator. Third in the league table come Midlanders and the Welsh with only 20 per cent stretching their muscles as often as the others.

The young and fit produce the nation's major sportsmen and women. Half the under 25's play sport very regularly and another quarter join in at sometime.

The poor are less sporty than the better off. Having lots of time on their hands does not seem to inspire the unemployed to be active in sport. They are much less likely than those in full-time work to be playing games. Many spend their leisure time kicking their heels instead of kicking a ball.

HOW OFTEN, IF AT ALL, DO YOU PARTICIPATE IN ANY FORM OF SPORT AS A PLAYER, NOT AS A SPECTATOR?

	%
Once a week or more often	**26**
Twice a month	**3**
Once a month	**4**
Less often	**8**
Never	**59**

EATING

Is there such a thing as a normal diet? It seems not. But there are definite changes occurring in patterns of eating habits.

Almost a third of us, for example, say we are deliberately eating less red meat compared with a quarter adopting this course of action a couple of years earlier. And the bad news for butchers is that women are far more likely than men to abandon the beef.

Fried and fatty foods are also getting the chop by almost half the nation. So too are sugar and salt.

So what are we filling up on? Four out of ten of us are eating more fruit, vegetables and high fibre foods.

And when we dive into the fruit bowl, what are we most likely to choose? If you take an apple you are normal. Over four out of five say it is their favourite fruit.

Next in popularity is a banana, followed by oranges, grapes and pears.

Which fruit do we think does us the most good? Almost everyone agrees apples and oranges. Bananas are in third place, followed by melons, pineapples, strawberries, avocados and Kiwi-fruit.

It's quite normal to demand variety in our diet, but do we choose our food for its taste or goodness?

Almost two thirds list taste as their top priority with only a fifth going for food that is good for them.

The food you choose also relates to your class. Pates, prawn cocktails and croissants are definitely upper and middle crust for example, while fish and chips, Black Forest gateau and sauce in bottles, are thought to be fodder for the working classes so if you ever get to dine among the tiaras and do not want to reveal your council house origins, avoid asking for the "Daddies".

What is normal about the most basic of all food, bread? For most of us bread is still the staff of life with 85 per cent of the population saying they bite a slice every day of the week. Half of the nation say they eat brown or wholemeal loaves most often and another third are conscious of the fibre argument and eat high-fibre white.

And although the traditional British sandwich-shaped loaf is most popular, it is the famous French stick that tops the polls when we shop for Continental and other foreign bread with half the nation preferring the Gallic approach compared with one in ten who go for the Greek pitta bread.

And if you always reach for the wrapped sliced loaf the rest assured you are among the majority, for six out of ten of us prefer our bread in this form.

Ready-sliced bread is the nation's favourite for making sandwiches with half the population preferring the convenience of not having to wield the bread knife or saw. And on the subject of sandwiches, nine out of ten of us prefer to make our own. And if you are Scottish, then you are even more likely to make your own. Could it be you Scots are keen to save a few extra pence in the process?

Is it normal to mop up gravy with bread? Nearly two thirds do, so are you among them?

If you are in the lower income groups you are far more likely than the rich to polish the plate in this manner.

The class divide also extends to those other great British table traditions dunking bread in soup and dipping bread soldiers in a boiled egg.

How many of us still eat breakfast? Two out of three say yes, but only one in seven opt for something cooked.

If you do eat breakfast, it is likely to be a lonely meal. Half of us eat it on our own, but tune into the radio for company. A quarter switch on the television or read a newspaper to accompany the tea and toast.

If you do happen to share breakfast with a partner, it is unlikely to produce a lively conversation. Only one in five elects to converse with our other half.

Breakfast is marginally more popular at weekends, presumably because we have more time, and a third indulge in a cooked breakfast with a fifth eating it in bed on Sundays.

And if you are in this category then you are more likely to be found living in the North West where almost one in three don't mind crumbs between the sheets.

And on the subject of Sundays, almost two thirds of the nation still insist on a traditional roast for lunch.

When do we start or stop eating?

Three-quarters of the nation wakes up before 7.30am. so we can safely assume that the majority of toasters are popping by 8.00am.

When it comes to the midday meal the term lunch-hour becomes something of a misnomer. Two-thirds eat between noon and 1.00pm. with three-quarters stopping for only half an hour.

THINKING OF MEALS AT HOME, HOW OFTEN DO YOU USUALLY EAT BREAD WITH YOUR MAIN MEAL? WOULD YOU SAY...

	%
Often	26
Sometimes	37
Never	37

WHEN EATING BREAD WITH YOUR MAIN MEAL, DO YOU EVER USE BREAD TO MOP UP YOUR GRAVY?

	%
Yes	58
No	42

WHICH OF THESE DO YOU USUALLY EAT OR DRINK AT LUNCH ON A WEEKDAY?

	%
Meat	33
Fish	21
Potatoes	24
Other vegetables	25
Salad	23
Bread	22
Water	4
Cheese	22
Fresh fruit	20
Tea	42
Coffee	30
Soup	14
Wine	1
Eggs	11
Crisps	8
Sandwiches	47
Beer	4
Sweets, chocolates	4
None of these	5

DRINKING

Each normal person needs at least a litre of liquid a day to survive. But how, when and what we swallow varies according to our sex, or job, the part of the country we live in, and how rich we are.

Low-cost tap water is the most popular thirst quencher - little wonder the Government is scrambling to privatise the whole business. But what about the alternatives? Tea, coffee, cola, beer, wine?

This is where fashion comes into play.

Wine is probably the most fashionable drink in the UK at the moment with 86 per cent of the nation giving it an "In" vote. It is closely followed by coffee, then tea, with mineral water and low-alcohol beer tying for fourth place. That other old-fashioned favourite, lemonade is definitely out, with only 48 per cent of the nation regarding it as fashionable drink.

The British also think it is fashionable to drink in wine bars with threequarters of the adult population voting them the place to be. Little wonder that the consumption of wine continues to rise and that wine now equals beer as our favourite form of alcohol. So if your tipple is a glass of red plonk, relax you're normal.

We all know we need to drink. But when does the swallowing start? What is the normal person's first drink of the day? Tea, upon awakening or for breakfast, is tops for seven out of ten of us, with coffee appealing to less than one in three.

At lunchtime, confusingly known as dinner-time by many, tea remains our favourite drink, but by then, a third of us have switched either to coffee, wine, water or beer.

Once back home in the evening, one in ten of us has an alcoholic drink before the evening meal but, bad news for licensees, only three per cent go for another drink at a pub.

What alcohol you drink often depends upon class. Champagne, cocktails and cognac are definitely seen as a tipple for toffs, while Guinness, stout, tea and instant coffee, refreshes the parts of the working classes. And if you want to spot a member of the middle class then look out for the wine-drinker or someone clutching a Martini, Bacardi or even a Babycham.

On a more serious note, North Americans put health warning notices on bottles of alcoholic drinks. What about alcohol use and abuse?

If you think that heavy drinking is a serious social problem then join the other 90 per cent of the population. In spite of the millions of gallons poured daily down thirsty British throats, as a nation we give the thumbs down to the bottoms up.

How far does our concern about the demon drink extend? Well, would you for example approve or disapprove of warnings about drinking excessive amounts of alcohol being printed on advertisements and labels on bottles of booze?

The chances are that you will approve of the idea because over 80 per cent vote in favour of this course of action.

If you drink alcohol what is your own favourite tipple? The average British man goes for beer and lager - seven pints a week of the foaming fizz, while women show a preference for wine.

DO YOU THINK THAT HEAVY DRINKING OF ALCOHOL IS A VERY SERIOUS PROBLEM IN THIS COUNTRY TODAY, A MODERATELY SERIOUS PROBLEM, NOT VERY SERIOUS, OR NOT REALLY A PROBLEM AT ALL?

	%
Very serious	50
Moderately serious	37
Not very serious	10
Not a problem	3

WOULD YOU PPROVE OR DISAPPROVE IF WARNINGS ABOUT DRINKING EXCESSIVE AMOUNTS OF ALCOHOL WERE PRINTED ON EVERY BOTTLE OF WINE, BEER AND SPIRIT AND ON EVERY ADVERTISEMENT FOR ALCOHOL?

	%
Approve	82
Disapprove	11
Don't know	7

RESTAURANTS

What is your favourite restaurant?

For most people it is the traditional English restaurant. Four out of ten make this their first choice.

English restaurants are even more popular among the elderly but less so among the young.

If you live in the North East, you are far more likely than average to choose an English restaurant, although once over the border, Scots reject Sassenach style, and are far less likely than average to venture into a restaurant serving 'English' style food.

It seems the younger or wealthier you are, the more adventurous the choice of restaurant.

Chinese restaurants are the second most popular choice especially among the young, where their popularity rises to capture a third of the 16-24 year vote.

The older you are, the less likely you are to call for the chopsticks and rice. Only five per cent of over 65's place a Chinese restaurant as their second choice.

The Chinese challenge varies from North to South. A quarter of Scots make them their second favourite, while East Anglians award them well below average marks.

What's next in the gastronomic league table? Italian, closely followed by Indian, with French cuisine dropping in at fifth place.

But although Greek restaurants score well among Londoners and East Anglians, they languish at the bottom of the national league table along with Spanish and Japanese.

Not surprisingly, the wealthy consistently place above-average votes for foreign restaurants, and are twice as likely as the average person to visit a French restaurant.

But many of us do not necessarily want to sit down under soft lights and be surrounded by singing waiters. We prefer take-away meals.

Our favourite take-away meal? You guessed it. Fish'n'Chips.

This original British take-away is voted No.1 by 30 per cent of the British. Chinese is a close second with curry another hot favourite in third place. Pizzas, kebabs and hamburgers are next in the take-away popularity poll.

But where you live makes a difference which take-away you prefer.

In Wales and the South West for example, Chinese take-away meals are far more popular than fish'n'chips.

Yorkshire folk, Geordies and the population of the South West, are above average lovers of fish'n'chips.

How old you are, also matters. Young adults are twice as likely to choose Hamburgers rather than fish'n'chips, while pensioners vote overwhelmingly for the great British favourite.

WHICH OF THESE IS YOUR FAVOURITE TAKE AWAY MEAL?

	%
Fish 'n' chips	30
Chinese	28
Curry	10
Pizza	8
Kebab	5
Hamburger	4
None of these	15

WHICH, IF ANY, OF THESE IS YOUR FAVOURITE TYPE OF RESTAURANT?

	%
English	42
Chinese	18
Italian	12
Indian	10
French	8
Greek	2
Spanish	1
Japanese	1
None of these	6

CLOTHES

No wonder the mini-skirt has made a comeback. Almost two thirds of all men say they prefer women's hemlines to end at the knee, or above it.

But if you have to wear a mini, then it's a very different story. Only one in ten women prefer to show lots of leg. In the 16-34 age group however, a third of the nation enjoys the idea of a breeze on the knees. But in spite of the majority of women's reluctance to wear a mini skirt, a quarter of the nation's females admit to wearing one in the past year.

If you are in favour of shocking stockings, where should you start looking? Try the lower middle class. They are well above- average in their preference for short skirts. For the prudish, look out for expensively dressed women, or pensioners, they are least likely to show off their knees.

Is it normal to be interested in fashion? The nation is evenly divided. Half say they pay attention to trends in women's fashion. And the other half say they do not. If you are 16-34 then your interest in the subject will rise considerably.

How normal are you when shopping for shoes? The chances are you will not be in a very good mood, for even the footwear retailers admit that buying shoes is a "stress purchase".

Apparently six times more people like shopping for clothes rather than shoes.

Almost three-quarters prefer self-selection, as opposed to help from an assistant when buying footwear. And four out of five 16- 24 year olds prefer self-selection. Four in ten of the elderly favour help.

Do you have difficulty in finding a pair of shoes that fit? A third of the population say they encounter difficulty in finding the correct length or width of shoes. It's a problem for four out of ten women, while men are less likely to have cause for complaint, only a quarter say they cannot find any comfortable shoes.

If you own a pair of trainers, whether you are nine or 90, you are quite normal. Two thirds of the nation now own at least one pair and this type of comfortable, leisure footwear is even popular among the old, with two in five pensioners owning a pair. In fact, 15 per cent of the nation's senior citizens own two or more pairs.

Where did you buy your last pair of shoes?

Two thirds say a shoe-shop, followed by chain stores, department stores and mail-order.

Women and shoppers in the 35-64 bracket are more likely to use chain stores, while the young and the lower income groups are least likely to buy their shoes from this type of outlet.

But never mind what the fashion pundits may be telling us about what's new, what clothes do we think are "in" and "out"?

Top of the "in" list with 85 out of every 100 votes are blue jeans. On and on they march as new generations follow their parents in declaring their popularity. Blue jeans are classless, ageless and international.

Next on the fashion list are mini skirts. Regardless of how many women actually wear them, they are "in" as far as most people are concerned.

In the underwear department boxer shorts are still "in" and Bermuda shorts are also given a 50 per cent "in" vote.

But if you want to spot who is really "out" - look out for a woman dressed in a real fur coat wearing a hat and leg warmers. All these items are top of the "out" list.

Should you see such a woman, she will probably be with a man wearing a bow tie, cuff links, Y-fronts, and a hat - all at the top of the men's "out" list.

By the way, you will also be able to recognise him by his pierced ears. They're "out" too!

THERE'S BEEN A LOT OF TALK RECENTLY ABOUT THE LENGTH OF WOMEN'S SKIRTS. WHAT DO YOU PREFER - HEMLINES THAT ARE ABOVE THE KNEE, AT THE KNEE OR BELOW THE KNEE?

	%
Above	22
At the knee	25
Below	35
Don't care	14
Don't know	4

LIFE

Birth

Death

Health

Weight

Rude Habits

Worries

BIRTH

It may be possible in the future to choose the sex of a child before birth, but do we want to?

85 per cent of men and women agree that they would rather leave the matter to chance. The younger you are then the more likely you are to leave the choice in the hands of Mother Nature.

The rich, more than any other income group would like to be able to determine in advance the sex of their unborn child.

People living in Wales, Scotland and the Midlands are nearly twice as likely as those living in the north of England to want to choose in advance which sex their children would be.

But does the father like to be present at the birth?

Yes, say four out of five modern young men. But only one in 17 of their grandfathers saw their children being born. This compares with half of today's under 25 year old men who were present when their children were born.

Scotsmen are the most likely of all British males to think that giving birth is womens' only business. Men from the South are more likely to be single or have no children but of those that do then half of them were present at the birth of their babies.

What do the mothers think about the father watching them give birth? Almost two thirds of women say they want the father to witness the birth of their child.

The rich and poor women were not as keen as the middle classes for Dad to be standing by the delivery table.

Women in the Midlands and Wales differed from those living in the rest of the country. Two out of five in these areas said they did not want the father present at the crucial moment.

Even though the majority of men say they want to see their children born, of those men with children, less than half were present for the event.

IF YOU WERE TO BECOME A FATHER, WOULD YOU WANT TO WITNESS THE BIRTH?

	%
Yes	64
No	29
Don't know	7

HAVE YOU EVER HAD ANY CHILDREN? DID YOU WITNESS THE BIRTH?

	%
No children	39
Yes, witnessed	25
No, didn't	36

WHAT DO YOU THINK IS THE IDEAL SIZE OF A FAMILY - HUSBAND, WIFE AND HOW MANY CHILDREN?

	%
None	1
One	3
Two	63
Three	14
Four or more	12
Don't know	7

DEATH

Who would like to live to the ripe old age of 150? Less than half of us apparently. With men, more than women, expressing such a hope.

Life is sweet apparently for the young, though with 43 per cent of 18 - 34 year olds saying that if science made it possible to live to 150 keeping all their strengths, they would like to live that long.

The fear of loneliness and the joy of family happiness emerged as the greatest issues about old age. Women are more frightened than men about loneliness in old age, whereas men are more concerned than women about tranquility, peace and personal fulfilment.

Is their life after death?

A quarter believe in reincarnation and one in six feel they have been in the presence of someone who has already died.

Has the contact anything to do with religion? Three out of five people do not feel it is a religious experience, although it had occured when they were completely alone.

It has been suggested that the laws should be changed so that doctors can be allowed to end the life of their patients, provided their patients agree.

What is the nation's reaction to such a proposal?

Almost two thirds approve of such a suggestion, although over 65's react with less than average enthusiasm to the idea.

Have you ever, even for a short time - seriously wished you were dead? No, say a resounding four in five. And of those who thought momentarily that life on earth was no longer for them, over 4 in 5 were glad their thoughts had not been translated into reality.

Medical miracles, however, are not so commonplace. Only one in ten say they know someone in their family given a short time to live, who recovered.

Should a person be able to end another's life?

If a person has an incurable disease and is very ill and unable to give his consent to have his life ended, do you think that doctors should or should not be allowed to end his life provided that his next of kin agree?

Over half of us think that doctors should be able to end someone's pain peacefully.

But what about the practical aspects of death. Wills, or lack of them, and funerals, are morbid subjects but what is normal?

Half the nation's over 60 year-olds have not made a will and nearly one in five say they worry about the cost of their funeral.

Asked about the cost of a funeral - reckoned to average around £750 - a third thought it was less than this amount and a quarter had no idea. Do people have enough money or insurance to pay for their funeral? Three quarters say yes, they have.

HAVE YOU EVER-EVEN IF ONLY FOR A SHORT TIME-SERIOUSLY WISHED YOU WERE DEAD?

	%
Yes	**20**
No	**79**
Can't remember	**1**

IF SCIENCE MADE IT POSSIBLE FOR YOU TO LIVE TO 150, KEEPING ALL YOUR STRENGTHS, WOULD YOU LIKE TO LIVE THAT LONG OR NOT?

	%
Yes I'd like to	**39**
It depends	**7**
No - I'd rather not	**51**
Don't know	**3**

IF A PERSON HAS AN INCURABLE DISEASE AND IS VERY ILL AND UNABLE TO GIVE HIS CONSENT TO HAVE HIS LIFE ENDED, DO YOU THINK THAT DOCTORS SHOULD OR SHOULD NOT BE ALLOWED TO END HIS LIFE PROVIDED THAT HIS NEXT-OF-KIN AGREE?

	%
Yes, doctors should be allowed	**69**
No, doctors should not	**22**
Don't know	**9**

HEALTH

What is the greatest health problem facing the nation at present? AIDS? Cancer? Heart disease?

If you gave your vote to any of these killers you would be wrong, for most people feel the greatest threat is the state of the National Health Service. And if you are in the 35-44 age group then it's likely to raise an even bigger problem in your mind.

We believe it needs more money, shorter waiting-lists and more nursing staff in that order.

What about the doctors? Do they do a good job or not?

If you believe your doctor does a good job then you, are normal, for over three-quarters of the adult population hold this view. An overwhelming 76 per cent think their doctor gives enough time to their treatment.

Have you ever asked him or her to visit you at night? Yes say 38 per cent.

Did you get the feeling he or she minded? No respond 81 per cent.

Conclusion? It is normal to receive satisfaction from your GP. Indeed, when quizzed about their services, two thirds of patients said their doctors started surgery hours on time, and 84 per cent were satisfied by the conditions in the waiting room.

But even with this satisfactory service, we still change our doctor from time to time, excluding the occasion when we move or our doctor moves. Two thirds of us have changed doctors at least once and a fifth of us have swopped three times or more.

What about treatment in hospital?

Nine out of ten are satisfied with the treatment and the nursing staff. Two-thirds think the food is fine, and four out of five are satisfied with hospital cleanliness and accommodation.

Would we be prepared to pay something towards the cost of a stay in hospital? Certainly, say half the nation.

Who swallows pills?

Nearly half the nation takes some form of medicine in any one week.

With over half of women compared with 41% of men taking some form of medication. Seven out of ten pensioners take some type of medicine compared with less than four in ten of the 18 to 34 year-old group.

The less well-off are more likely than the middle classes and the rich to need medicine.

Finally, many of us are ignorant about the most elementary facts to do with our bodies. Would you believe it is normal not to know where the liver is to be found?

WHAT WOULD YOU SAY IS THE MOST URGENT HEALTH PROBLEM FACING THIS COUNTRY AT THE PRESENT TIME?

	%
The NHS	33
Aids	25
Cancer	16
Heart Diseaes	7
Drug/Drug abuse	1
Drink/Alcohol Abuse	1
Old people	1
Other	6
Don't know	10

IN GENERAL, WOULD YOU SAY YOUR DOCTOR DOES A GOOD JOB OR A POOR JOB?

	%
Good	78
Fair	12
Poor	6
Don't know	4

WEIGHT

How would you like to lose a few pounds...of weight that is? Over half of us think we are overweight and the average amount we would like to lose is 19lbs. If all those weight-loss wishes came true then the average man would end up weighing 10st. 8lbs and the average woman 7st. 8lbs.

But what is normal? It depends on how tall you are, but the weight of the average British man is 11st.13lbs. with the average female weighing in at exactly two stones lighter at 9st.13lbs.

And if 44 million adult Britons all achieved their aim, a staggering 836 million pounds of flab or 373,000 tons would disappear.

Who wants to lose weight the most?

Women are more conscious of the problem than men. It's an ambition of two-thirds of women compared with a third of men.

Regionally, Scots think they have the biggest weight problem.

The Welsh and Midlanders are least likely to want to shed a few pounds.

The dreaded middle-age spread is clearly confirmed with the 35-65 year olds weighing in at least five pounds or so above the national average. At the other end of the social spectrum, the young and poor tip the scales marginally below the national average.

Northerners are marginally heavier than Southerners but for real roly-polys go to Scotland - where you are likely to find twice the national average of people weighing over 15 stones. Well over half of all Scots say they would dearly love to shed a few pounds.

Interestingly, 45 per cent of the nation is quite satisfied with its present weight, while seven per cent of skinnies actually want to put a few pounds on.

DO YOU KNOW HOW MUCH YOU WEIGH?

	Men %	Women %
Up to 7 stones	0	8
8 stones - under 9	2	17
9 stones - under 10	6	18
10 stones - under 11	19	17
11 stones - under 12	22	10
12 stones - under 13	19	7
13 stones - under 14	11	1
14 stones - under 15	7	3
15 stones or over	7	1
Don't know	7	17

WOULD YOU LIKE TO LOSE WEIGHT, PUT ON WEIGHT OR STAY AS YOU ARE?

	Men %	Women %
Lose	33	61
Put on	9	5
Stay same	58	32
Don't know	0	2

HOW MUCH WOULD YOU LIKE TO LOSE IN LBS?

	Men %	Women %
Up to 3 lbs	2	2
4 - 5 lbs	3	3
6 - 7 lbs	16	21
8 - 9 lbs	3	8
10 - 11 lbs	3	1
12 - 13 lbs	1	0
1 stone	35	22
1st 1lb - 1st 7lbs	12	6
Over $1^1/_2$ - Under 2 stones	1	1
2 sts - 2st 6lbs	14	19
2sts 7lbs or more	7	12
Don't know	2	4

RUDE HABITS

Some sports people, especially footballers had better watch out. It is not so much the ability to kick the ball, punch an opponent or make rude signals to the referee. No, the action that is causing the nation concern is...spitting in public.

Spitting has been singled out as the most objectionable personal habit in Britain, with almost a third of us placing it at the top of the anti-social league table.

It comes well before body smells mentioned by a quarter of the nation, nose-picking, biting fingernails, belching, bad breath or even breaking wind in the company of others.

Strangely enough, tolerance to what are mostly normal bodily functions, changes, depending upon how old you are, where you live and what you do for a living.

Take breaking wind for example. The further north you live, the less likely this particular social grace, or lack of it, is likely to offend those in the immediate vicinity.

Southerners and the well-off are most likely to turn up their noses. Whereas people with lower incomes living in the Midlands, Wales and Scotland have a far higher tolerance level and are least affected by the habit.

Could it be that those brisk northerly winds provide the perfect antidote to the human variety?

Then there is the sexual divide. Women, for example, find nose picking and breaking wind in public far more objectionable than men do. Surprisingly, bad breath and belching on the other hand are less likely to cause annoyance.

As far as age is concerned, it is the 45 year olds and over who hate the spitting habit the most. Young people who have been brought up to accept the use of deodorants and perfume from an early age are more likely to put evil body odours at the top of their list. Then again, the poorer you are the more you are likely to dislike nose-pickers.

So if you hate people who spit, smell and pick their nose in public, join the majority. On the other hand, if you happen to be one of the offenders perhaps a pack of tissues and a soap-on- a-rope could put you back on the path to personal pleasantness?

WHICH OF THESE PERSONAL HABITS DO YOU FIND MOST OBJECTIONABLE?

	%
Picking nose	**15**
Breaking wind in public	**11**
Spitting	**31**
Belching	**3**
Bad breath	**9**
Biting finger nails	**4**
Smelly body odour	**25**
None of these	**3**

WORRIES

If you worry, are you normal? And if you do worry, how much do you worry? And what do you worry about?

Most of us it seems are worriers. Only a quarter of the nation is totally relaxed and doesn't worry at all. The younger you are, then the greater the chance you are a worrier.

Our number one worry is money. Seven out of ten people worry about making both ends meet, and not surprisingly almost half the lower income groups and a third of people under 35, worry about their lack of cash a great deal. Having enough money in old age is a great worry for those approaching retirement but interestingly, once retired, the worry about lack of money diminishes rapidly.

Next on our list of worries? More than half the nation worries about health with a third of young people very concerned about the issue. Only a quarter of the over 65's worry a lot about their health.

The need for a decent home comes high on the list of worries, with half the nation saying they worry about having a reasonable place to live. The scale of this concern rises dramatically among the young but it is only a worry for a quarter of the retired.

In this age of rapid redundancy are you normal to worry about losing your job? Almost half do, and if you are in the middle income bracket the answer is far more likely to be yes.

What else worries us? The possibility of another war concerns four out of ten, as does the possibility of not getting proper food.

After personal problems, what international issues present normal cause for concern?

The destruction of the ozone layer is top of a frightening list of issues and understandably it is of greater-than-average concern among young adults. Nuclear power and presumably the possibility of accidents such as those in the USA and USSR, are high on the list of worries.

And after widespread publicity, the threat of food poisoning is third on the list of worst worries with women voicing above average concern.

What brings peace of mind and a perfect world for normal worriers?

Television, computers, religion, factories and democracy are regarded as essential by half the nation.

Loneliness, unemployment, crime and exploitation are considered to be the least desirable aspects of society.

Having decided what we need in a perfect world, which disasters do we think are likely to occur in the next decade?

City riots are among our concerns. So too is political terrorism and the view that the police will find it impossible to protect our personal safety on the streets.

Less than one in ten citizens believe there is any likelihood of the Government being overthrown by revolution.

In our state of anxiety, do we believe that the people running the country care about us?

Six in ten consider that they do not care what happens to us. And an even greater percentage feel that most people with power try to take advantage of the rest of us.

IN GENERAL, HOW MUCH WOULD YOU SAY YOU WORRY - A LOT, A FAIR AMOUNT, A LITTLE OR NOT AT ALL?

	%
A lot	18
A fair amount	24
A little	33
Not at all	24
Don't know	1

WHICH OF THESE ISSUES CONCERNS YOU MOST?

	%
Ozone layer	23
Nuclear power	19
Food poisoning	13
Rain forests	13
Water pollution	8
Air pollution	8
Litter	8
Acid rain	2
None of these	6

LUCK

Horoscopes

Superstitions

Happiness

Gambling

HOROSCOPES

If you read your horoscope in a newspaper or magazine, do you believe what it predicts? Almost three in four of us say we don't believe what the stargazers forecast, with less than one in four believing the advice on what the future holds.

Women are twice as likely as men to believe what they read about their "stars". And the young, 18-34 year olds, are more likely than the over 65's to believe in their future fortunes as predicted by the multitude of astrologers.

Liberals are far more likely than Conservatives to believe in the idea of horoscopes. But upper income groups place rather less reliance on the outcome of the forecasts than those in the lower- income bracket, who tend to place above-average faith in the predictions.

Most people in Britain think these characteristics of their birth sign sums up their personality:-

DEC 23 - JAN 19 CAPRICORN
Careful, ambitious, witty, mean, pessimistic, rigid.

JAN 20 - FEB 19 AQUARIUS
Independent, original, peverse, obstinate.

FEB 20 - MAR 21 PISCES
Intuitive, kind, vague, weak-willed.

MAR 22 - APR 20 ARIES
Energetic, brave, direct, impatient, selfish, unsubtle.

APR 21 - MAY 21 TAURUS
Warm, determined, stubborn, possessive.

MAY 22 - JUNE 22 GEMINI
Lively, versatile, superficial, inconsistent.

JUNE 23 - JULY 23 CANCER
Kind, imaginative, sensitive, over emotional, unforgiving, moody.

JULY 24 - AUG 23 LEO
Strong, generous, creative, intolerant, pompous, conceited.

AUG 24 - SEPT 23 VIRGO
Modest, practical, aloof, fussy, over-critical.

SEPT 24 - OCT 23 LIBRA
Idealistic, charming, romantic, indecisive, lazy, frivolous.

OCT 24 - NOV 22 SCORPIO
Passionate, purposeful, subtle, jealous, secretive.

NOV 23 - DEC 22 SAGITTARIUS
Optimistic, active, tactless, restless, irresponsible.

Pisces men and Sagittarius women dislike their characteristics most, followed by Libra and Pisces women.

Taurus the bull sign, was the most popular of the heavenly characteristics, with three quarters of people born under this sign saying that they thought the words which summed them up were perfectly suited.

Next in the satisfaction league came Cancer with 74 per cent and then Aquarius with 73 per cent.

DO YOU BELIEVE IN HOROSCOPES?

	%
Yes	**23**
No	**72**
Don't know	**5**

SUPERSTITIONS

When you see a ladder in the street do you walk round it? Half the nation does, so are you one of them?

Oddly enough, although only a quarter of the nation admits to being superstitious, one in two touches wood for good luck and admits to throwing salt over the shoulder for the same reason.

But superstitions apart, walking under ladders is not so much to do with encouraging good luck as discouraging bad luck. After all, it is easy to spot how to avoid a falling window cleaner, painter or roof repairer to say nothing of the paint, water, tiles or hammer! Simply give the ladder a wide birth.

Women are more superstitious than men, and young adults are more superstitious than their grandparents. Perhaps time and longevity induces the belief that luck is in everyone's own hands?

But what do the superstitious believe in? How do you react to the following situations. A black cat; Friday the 13th; putting new shoes on a table; breaking a mirror; a single magpie; crossed knives; touching wood; passing on stairs; opening an umbrella indoors; killing a spider?

Less than ten per cent of the superstitious in our society say they believe in any one of these events, which seems to indicate that although we all acknowledge the threat, most people dismiss the forecasted outcome.

Or could there be a more practical solution to some of the more bizarre superstitions?

Could it be, for example, that the reason women outnumber men, three to one in thinking that new shoes on the table brings bad luck, is simply because they buy more shoes than men?

ARE THERE ANY SUPERSTITIONS THAT YOU BELIEVE IN?

	%
Yes	**26**
No	**74**

HAPPINESS

How happy are we with our lives? Pretty content by all accounts. Eighty-six per cent of us say we are very, moderately or quite satisfied with our lives.

Young people (16-29 years olds) have marginally below average levels of satisfaction, but 30-44 year olds say they are most content and register well above average levels of satisfaction.

Why should this be? Well, for a start almost three-quarters of us say we are either living well, with enough income or coping with present earnings.

Six in ten of us are satisfied with the work we do, but eight in ten are unhappy about standards of honesty and behaviour.

Marriage provides a great deal of contentment, with almost eight in ten married couples confirming they are very satisfied with married life.

How does happiness show through? Singing out loud or humming a tune is one example. Four in five Britons sing to themselves at some time and two in five sing every day.

How do you rate on the satisfaction scale compared to your fellow Britons?

For example, are you satisfied with the amount of leisure and free time you get to yourself? Are you satisfied with your housing situation? What about the standard of living of yourself and your family - satisfied or dissatisfied?

If your answer to the first three questions is yes, then compared with the rest of the country you are normal. Three quarters of the nation say they are satisfied.

Almost two thirds are satisfied with their work and more than half the country claims to be satisfied with their family income and the future facing themselves and their families.

But what are some of the things we are most dissatisfied about? Childrens' education is one subject which divides the nation equally. With as many people (40%) declaring that they are dissatisfied as those that think their child's education is satisfactory.

The position of Britain in the world today worries more than half the residents of the country. But the subject which unites the country as a major dissatisfaction is the honesty and standard of behaviour of the people around them. 84 per cent of the nation said that they were dissatisfied with this aspect of British life.

How satisfied are you with your husband or wife? Very satisfied, fairly satisfied or not very satisfied?

Of all the married people asked, 79 per cent said that they were very satisfied.

HOW SATISFIED ARE YOU WITH THE WAY IN WHICH YOUR CHILD(REN) IS (ARE) BEING EDUCATED?

	%
Very satisfied	35
Fairly satisfied	37
Not very satisfied	18
Very dissatisfied	9
Don't know	1

HOW SATISFIED WOULD YOU GENERALLY SAY YOU WERE WITH YOUR LIFE?

	%
Very satisfied	25
Moderately satisfied	33
Quite satisfied	28
Not very satisfied	10
Not at all satisfied	4

GAMBLING

Every normal person has a flutter now and then? Not true.

Over half the nation never bothers. Not even with a raffle ticket or premium bond. But a third bet regularly, most often on the football pools.

The vast majority who bet on the pools do so every week. The poorer you are, the greater the likelihood to fill in a coupon every week in an attempt to get rich quick. Men are more likely than women to fill in football pool coupons. So too are the middle-aged. The rich and the young are least likely to be tempted.

Only one in eight bets on horses, and although horse racing is the sport of Kings, it is the lower income groups who are most likely to gamble on the nags.

So if the turf attracts you, where are you most likely to place your bet? High Street bookmakers are the most popular choice but are a male domain. For every woman popping in to place a bet, she is likely to be outnumbered by four men.

Apart from bingo, women are less attracted to the thrill of winning or losing than men. They gamble on horses less than once a month, and then it is usually a flutter on a big race such as the Grand National or the Derby.

For women, bingo is the most attractive way to gamble. They are twice as likely to play bingo than bet with a bookmaker. Senior citizens dip into their purses and hopefully shout "House" more regularly than most.

The third most popular form of gambling is a game of cards or dice. Cards are as popular among women as men and brag, pontoon and poker players are more than likely to be young.

What about "Ernie"? Four in ten have bought Premium Bonds, with the elderly and wealthy being above average owners. The young and less well-heeled are least likely to have had a go on the Government's gamble.

Only three in a hundred go to casinos or gambling clubs, and even fewer go to the races and bet with an on-course bookmaker.

Our opinion of newspaper race tipsters reveals that although one in five think they may be "fairly good", the majority either think "they are not at all good", "don't know" or "don't care".

Of the people who had gambled in the past 12 months, only one in six thought they had broken even, while seven in ten said they lost.

WHICH, IF ANY, OF THE FOLLOWING DO YOU EVER DO THESE DAYS?

Go in for the football pools	34
Use betting shops or off-course bookmaker	12
Go to bingo where admission charge is made	8
Playing cards or dice for money in places other than casino's	9
Put money on the tote	6
Use on-course bookmaker	2
Go to a gambling club or a casino	3
None of these	55

THINKING BACK OVER ALL THE BETS OF ANY KIND YOU HAVE PLACED OVER THE LAST 12 MONTHS, AND RECKONING YOUR WINNINGS AGAINST YOUR LOSSES, DID YOU BREAK EVEN OR HAVE YOU, ON BALANCE, LOST MONEY OR WON MONEY?

	%
Broke even	17
Lost money	68
Won money	11
Don't know	4

PEOPLE

Neighbours

Parents

Foreigners

Race

Class

Population

NEIGHBOURS

Do you get on with your neighbours? Four in five of us do, but almost a tenth say they never speak to the folks next door, with the young in particular declining to gossip over the garden fence, feed the pets or borrow a cup of sugar.

Where you live plays a part. As many Northerners have always believed, Southerners are more insular. Surveys confirm that Scots are more likely than most other regional groups to get on with their neighbours.

The degree of friendship becomes more fascinating because the rich rather than the poor are far more likely to get on extremely well with their neighbours. Where does this leave the notion of the under-priviledged clinging together for comradeship and support?

Senior citizens are the most likely age group to be friendly with their neighbours, with over nine in ten saying they have a good relationship with the people next door.

Women are marginally more likely than men to be able to claim they get on extremely well with their neighbours; presumably because they are more likely than men to be at home?

HOW WELL DO YOU GET ON WITH YOUR NEIGHBOURS?

	%
Extremely well	**43**
Reasonably well	**44**
Not very well	**4**
Never speak to them	**8**
Don't know	**1**

PARENTS

How well do you get on with your parents? Do they embarrass you?

Are there times when you cringe and wish they would shut up or go away?

The younger you are then the more likely it is that Mum or Dad do something in public which causes you to squirm.

Being nosey and arguing in front of other people are the two activities guaranteed to embarrass young people. Intolerance and bigotry is most embarrassing to the middle-aged and the richer you are, the more likely you are to be embarrassed by it.

Dancing parents, too much drinking and telling jokes all rate on the list of embarrassing parental activity.

However, the majority of us think today's youth has more freedom and greater independence than previous generations. They have more freedom of expression and choice, certainly more money and possibly, more style. Most people also agree that today's youngsters have a more open relationship with their parents.

Have times changed since the swinging sixties?

The easy-going nature of the decade, the belief in freedom, and the artistic and musical creativity all receive high marks.

But drugs and sexual freedom register as negative influences.

A generation later, drugs are still foremost in people's minds when asked for their impression of what is bad about the young people of the 'eighties. But sex has been pushed out of second place by violence and vandalism.

On the brighter side, today's independent young people are thought to be more mature than their parents at the same age. They have a greater awareness of reality, have the ability to speak their minds and are more concerned for others.

What do young people believe they do differently from their parents?

Drinking, disco's and night-clubs are considered to be normal pastimes and they watch more television and listen to more music than their parents.

Moral standards are different too, say three-quarters of the nation, with a quarter thinking their sexual attitudes are the same as their parents.

When asked to select from a list of ten subjects which things were important to them as youngsters, every age group agreed that first, everybody wants a good marriage. Next, they want their parents to be proud of them.

WHAT MOST EMBARRASSES YOU ABOUT YOUR PARENTS?

	%
Intolerant/bigotted	5
Too proud of me	2
Drink too much	2
When they tell jokes	1
When they dance	1
Being nosey	4
Behaviour with opposite sex/adultery	1
Act too young	1
Arguing in fron tof other people	5
Communication (or lack) about sexual matters	1
Other	12
Nothing	67
Don't know	4

FOREIGNERS

What does the normal person think about foreigners? And which nation does the average Briton trust?

In spite of major clashes in two world wars, a quarter of us believe that Germany is our best friend on the continent of Europe - with France only mustering 16 per cent of our votes and Holland five per cent. There was little enthusiasm for the friendship of our other EEC partners.

Men are far more strongly drawn towards Germany than women, with a third of them believing that their best EEC pals live there.

Offered the choice to live on the Continent, the most popular place to settle would be ... Germany. France comes second with Switzerland third. The sun-soaked Costas are favourite for one in ten, but the holiday paradise of Greece only rates a two per cent vote.

Should the opportunity arise for an all-expenses paid holiday to any European country, Switzerland emerges as the number one destination with almost a fifth choosing the land of the cuckoo clocks and clear, clean air.

The ability to understand what our Continental cousins are talking about could be another issue. According to our poll, it is certainly not normal to have an understanding of the local lingo.

When asked, "Do you speak any foreign languages sufficiently well to be able to make sense of a newspaper written in that language?" - the best the British could reply, was 15 per cent saying "yes" - to French!

Admittedly, the figure rose to reach 25 per cent among the higher income group, but it dipped badly at the other end of the social spectrum.

Six per cent say they can speak German and two per cent claimed a knowledge of Spanish.

In fact, rather than our EEC partners, we prefer the friendship of the USA. Three in four say they like Americans, but only three in five prefer the friendship of the French and Germans.

But who would we trust in the event of another war? Who would we welcome as an ally?

Over four in five agree that the Americans would make the most trustworthy partners. Next comes Germany getting three in four votes. For third choice we go to Norway and Denmark with France dropping in at number five.

The Mediterranean countries of Spain, Italy and Greece are considered to be the least trustworthy in such circumstances.

In matters of trade, the Empire still has a place in half of our hearts. Australia is the most trusted nation with Canada a close second. Germany emerges as the third most trusted trading partner but is a long way behind.

The USA is believed capable of fair play in business by almost a quarter of us but Russia, Japan and South Africa are viewed with most suspicion when it comes to trade. Indeed, when it comes to trading with the Japanese specifically, two-thirds of us don't believe that they will honour their word when it comes to opening up their own markets to British products.

But underneath all the suspicion and prejudice do we want to be more friendly?

Over half of us say our relationship with Russia and Eastern Europe for example is not close enough.

We are probably a bit too friendly with the USA say an almost equal number and two-thirds think our relationship with Germany is about right.

Which nation do we believe produces the highest quality goods? Germany, say six in ten, with an even greater number of men agreeing. Japan comes second, with half of the nation's vote, while Sweden and Switzerland capture third and fourth places.

IF YOU HAD TO LIVE ON THE CONTINENT, WHICH COUNTRY WOULD YOU CHOOSE?

Germany	17
France	13
Switzerland	11
Spain	9
Holland	8
Sweden	5
Italy	4
Belgium	4
Greece	2
Denmark	2
Norway	1
Other	7
Don't know	17

RACE

Are you racially prejudiced?

Four in ten say they are not at all prejudiced, but the remainder admit some degree of prejudice.

At one extreme, six per cent say they are "very prejudiced" and almost another fifth declare they are "fairly prejudiced".

Age has a bearing on racist attitudes. Older people for example, are more likely than average to hold racist views. While the least prejudiced are likely to be found among the under 25's.

The majority of people, four in five, acknowledge that discrimination exists because of peoples' colour or race. Men tend to be more racist than women and within the different income groups the lowest earners are the least prejudiced.

Regionally, people in the North are the least prejudiced followed by the Scots, the Welsh and Midlanders. Southerners are more racially prejudiced than any other regional group.

But the better educated you are, the less likely you are to be prejudiced.

If black or Asian people came to live next door to you would you move home?

While only one in 20 said they would move away, the majority (78 per cent) said they would stay where they are.

Different food and shopkeeping are seen as the main contributions of immigrants, with two in every five Britons admiring the hard working and ambitious attitudes of the Asian people living in Britain.

DO YOU THINK THERE IS OR IS NOT ANY DISCRIMINATION IN THIS COUNTRY TODAY AGAINST PEOPLE BECAUSE OF THEIR COLOUR OR RACE?

	%
Is	**80**
Is not	**17**
Don't know	**3**

CLASS

Is there still a class struggle in this country? Yes, say the majority of Britons. But while the struggle continues, it is clear that there have been significant shifts in the definition of the boundaries.

So which social class would you say you belong to? If you answer "Working-class", understandably, so do pensioners and lower-income groups.

Over a third of us say we belong to the middle classes with a higher than average number clustered among 30-44 year olds, high- income groups and home-owners.

Surprisingly, almost all the nation is reluctant to confess to being upper class.

But the new generation of British adults has shifted its class position from that of its parents. When asked, "Which class did your parents belong to when you were young"? Two-thirds said working-class and less than one in three said middle class.

And the older you are, the more likely you are to think that your parents were working-class.

Concerned about your popularity? Then relax if you are working-class, because this group is voted the class that is most liked by 57 per cent, as opposed to a 48 per cent vote for the middle class; and 21 per cent for the upper class.

The working-classes are most liked in Scotland and least liked in the South.

Most people are ambivalent about the upper classes while only one in four people say they like them, a similar percentage also dislikes them.

Is belonging to a social class still important and does it offer more chances in life for the average Briton? On average only 15 per cent believe this to be so. But a third of the well-off, who are most likely to be upper class, confirm this belief.

While only eight per cent of the lower income groups say this is the case.

What irritates us about the different classes?

A fifth of the nation is wound up by the working class's general complacency and tendency to blame everything on the Government, while another third level the criticisms of pretentiousness, arrogance and social climbing at the middle classes.

Snobbish behaviour, the adoption of a superior attitude, too much wealth and a distinct lack of understanding about how the other half lives, top the list of criticisms of the upper class. And these views are held even more strongly by the young and council-house tenants.

WHAT SOCIAL CLASS WOULD YOU SAY YOU BELONG TO?

	%
Upper class	0
Upper middle class	2
Middle class	36
Lower middle class	12
Working class	39
Don't believe in class	7
Don't know	4

FOR EACH OF THESE PEOPLE COULD YOU PLEASE TELL ME WHICH CLASS YOU THINK THEY BELONG TO

TWIGGY	
Upper class	9
Middle class	42
Working-class	42
Don't know	7
ARTHUR SCARGILL	
Upper class	5
Middle class	28
Working-class	62
Don't know	5
TERRY WOGAN	
Upper class	16
Middle class	65
Working-class	15
Don't know	7
MICHAEL PARKINSON	
Upper class	27
Middle class	53
Working-class	15
Don't know	5

POPULATION

How long is the average life span? Is it normal to expect to live to 80? And what are the chances of dying from old age?

Official population projections assume that a boy born at the present time can expect to live just over 75 years and a girl just over 80 years. Figures based on deaths in 1983 - 1985 were 71 years and 77 years respectively, whereas if they had been in the early years of the century life expectancies would have been 48 and 52 years respectively.

The number of people aged 65 or over has grown by 3.2 million since 1951 and is expected to increase by another 2.6 million by the year 2025. Those aged 65 to 74 are projected to make up over half of the population.

Do you think of yourself as being 'young'? Of course you do if you happen to actually be young, but it is still a normal feeling even if you are over 65. Six out of ten pensioners think of themselves as young. And so too do seven out of ten 55-64 year olds.

What do we do to keep looking and feeling young?

Keeping fit is a top priority, followed by eating properly, keeping happy, dressing fashionably and taking an interest in what is going on.

For some, retirement may seem a long way off, but more of us intend to retire well before we are 65. Almost one in ten are intent on putting our feet up by the time we reach 55 and a third intend to down tools by 60. And 20 years from now, four in ten believe they will have retired by the age of 55.

AGGRESSION

Terrorism

War

Crime

Hunting

Rows

Drugs

TERRORISM

Three in four of us would be happy to ban the private possession of guns. And women are far more emphatic than men that the Government should outlaw gun owners.

Regionally, North Country people are more likely to approve Parliamentary action against gun ownership than those living in the Midlands and Wales.

One in four of 16-24 year olds say they disapprove of their MPs voting against gun ownership, compared with one in ten of their parents.

WOULD YOU APPROVE OR DISAPPROVE IF PARLIAMENT WAS TO BAN THE PRIVATE POSSESSION OF ALL GUNS

	%
Approve	76
Disapprove	16
Don't know	8

WAR

How normal are you when it comes to a fight?

Would you stand up and fight for Queen and country in the event of another war?

Three in five of men under 35 say yes, but a fifth say no. However, were an invader to set foot on our shores, then half the objectors would change their minds, and join their comrades in arms.

In the event of invasion then four-fifths of Britain's young men would unite to defend their country.

But even in these circumstances a tenth still say they would not fight.

It is one thing defending the homeland but another fighting for allies. Only one in three men under 35 would fight alongside a foreign ally. Two in five would not help.

Only half of British men would be prepared to go to war with the Soviet Union or get involved in a war similar to the Falklands.

Over half the pacifists think there ought to be better ways to resolve international conflicts. A quarter believe that war is never justified and one in 20 are forbidden to fight - it's against their religious beliefs.

A third of British young men say they are as patriotic as other generations but over half felt differently from their fathers and grandfathers who fought and won two world wars. They believe their generation is less patriotic than other generations.

A third of the young are firmly convinced that the older folk have learned nothing at all from war. The lesson for a quarter of them is simply not to have another war.

Almost half the nation does not think there will be a Third World War, a view that is particularly strong among the young and lower income groups. But for those pessimists who do think there will be another world war, six in ten think it is at least ten years away.

And horror of horror, should it ever arrive, what sort of war will it be? Two thirds think nuclear, and a third say conventional weapons.

How will it start? By a conflict between other nations somewhere else in the world, say one in three. Deliberate aggression by one side or the other, or an accidental firing of a nuclear weapon, say a fifth.

Who would win an East-West conflict? Neither side, say almost half.

What about our defence? Most people vote for a mix of nuclear weapons and a strong conventional non-nuclear force.

Should we give up our nuclear weapons? No, say almost two-thirds.

Were we to be attacked by nuclear weapons should we respond immediately or get the agreement of our allies? Over half say seek agreement but a third say, reply with our weapons.

Having access to nuclear weapons is comforting for two thirds of the nation, and the fact that we have a nuclear capability, decreases the risk of nuclear attack, say almost half of us.

Were there to be a nuclear war affecting Britain what do we think would be our chances of survival? Extremely bad say almost nine in ten, with individual chances of survival rated as "poor".

WHO DO YOU THINK WOULD WIN IF IT CAME TO A WAR BETWEEN THE WEST AND RUSSIA?

	%
West	19
Russia	17
Nobody would win	47
Don't know	16

TO 16-34 YEAROLD MEN:
OF COURSE, WE ALL HOPE THAT THERE WILL NOT BE ANOTHER WAR BUT IF IT WERE TO COME TO THAT WOULD YOU BE WILLING TO FIGHT FOR YOUR COUNTRY?

	%
Yes	59
Depends on circumstances	15
No	20
Don't know	6

DO YOU THINK THAT YOUR GENERATION IS GENERALLY:

	%
More patriotic than other generations	6
Less patriotic than other generations	51
As patriotic as other generations	36
Don't know	7

CRIME

What are the odds on being burgled?

Although only 17 in a 100 people claim to have experienced this frightening event, three in five admit they fear it is their turn next.

The chances of being burgled rise significantly if you live in a detached house in Scotland or the North of England. The safest homes are terraced houses in the Midlands and Wales.

So what is normal as far as domestic security is concerned?

Two thirds of the nation's homes have two front and two back door locks. Just over half have window locks. But less than one in ten has a burglar alarm.

Burglar alarms are most likely to be found in Northern homes which is not surprising given the above average number of burglaries.

But how just is British justice? Over half the nation believes it favours the rich - a view held more strongly than average by men and middle-aged, middle class people, with two thirds saying that our system of law and justice is just not fair to everybody.

In fact, almost seven in ten believe that now and again there are cases where people are sent to prison for crimes they didn't commit.

What do we think about our guardians of peace, the police? Almost half of us think they are efficient and do a good job but almost as many believe they are responsible for scattered cases of corruption and violence. Do the Police have enough power or too much? How far are we prepared to let them go in their quest to prevent crime?

Two in three think they should be allowed to fingerprint everyone in an area where a serious crime has been committed.

Dispersing potentially violent demonstrators by using tear gas, water cannons or plastic bullets is also acceptable to more than two thirds. And over half the nation think that policemen or women should be allowed to stop and search anyone they think is suspicious.

The right to privacy is however important to three-quarters of the British. They do not want the police to have access to files containing information on citizens who don't have a criminal record. Nor do they think the police should be able to tap telephones or record private conversations.

Detaining subjects for more than 24 hours without charging them is frowned upon by two-thirds of the British. Nearly as many people believe that the police should not be able to question subjects before they have been allowed to consult a lawyer.

But few like the idea of our police carrying guns. Almost three in four reject the idea. Having said that, one in two think the Police use of firearms is about right and another quarter think they do not use their guns often enough - a view that is shared particularly by members of the Conservative Party, the young and the lower income groups.

Some people have suggested that the abolition of the right to remain silent would mean the end of a fundamental principle of British justice - that an accused person is innocent until proved guilty. If you believe this then join the other 56 per cent of the nation who think the same.

But crimes of violence are of increasing concern. The public was invited the public to list social problems in Britain. Top of the list came drugs, closely followed by rape and crimes of violence.

Retribution is a normal reaction to someone who has suffered from a criminal act, but what does the average person think should be the first concern of the courts in sentencing a criminal?

Punishment for what the guilty party has done to others, say two in five. Punishment, to act as a warning to others say another similar percentage. Only one in seven see the mission as one of salvation - "Do what we can to retain the offender as a good citizen," they say.

How effective is prison as a deterrent? And just how tough do we think life is behind bars?

Almost half imagine that life in prison is not all that hard on the criminals, but there is a sympathetic 12 per cent who feel that life inside is very hard on the prisoners.

How relaxed are you about letting "lifers" out on parole? Two thirds are against the idea with only one in six in favour of early release.

What is the average person's idea of a life sentence? Half think up to 20 years behind bars is a "life" sentence. One in ten say up to 24 years and just over one in five think up to 29 years should be served before parole is considered.

What should life inside be like for the prisoners? On balance we are in favour of them watching TV in their cells and particularly keen on them receiving professional training, taking examinations and participating in sports.

The idea of allowing a prisoner's partner to visit and enjoy making love, is definitely not on say two-thirds of the nation.

WHAT DO YOU THINK ABOUT THE POLICE'S USE OF FIREARMS THESE DAYS? DO YOU THINK THEY USE THEM TOO OFTEN OR NOT OFTEN ENOUGH?

	%
Too often	14
Not often enough	25
About right	54
Don't know	7

ARE YOU IN FAVOUR OR OPPOSED TO LETTING A PERSON SENTENCED TO LIFE IMPRISONMENT OUT ON PAROLE AFTER A CERTAIN NUMBER OF YEARS SERVED?

	%
In favour	17
Opposed	67
Don't know	16

HUNTING

The majority of British dislike the idea of hunting foxes, stags and hares, and two thirds of the nation say they would approve Government legislation forbidding blood sports. Even boxing is rejected by four in ten.

So where are the supporters of the hunt? Upper income groups and Conservative voters are least likely to want fox-hunting stopped, neither are the elderly that bothered. The young, and Liberal voters however, represent the sector of society that would most like the sport banned.

Hunting is most likely to be an upper class activity say almost nine in ten. Less than one in ten identified hunting with the middle class and the working class hardly registered a score. Clearly the sound of the huntsman's horn has still to awaken the interest of the majority of the British.

WITH WHICH CLASS DO YOU MOST ASSOCIATE HUNTING?

	%
Upper class	86
Middle class	7
Working-class	1
All	4
Don't know	2

WOULD YOU APPROVE OR DISAPPROVE IF PARLIAMENT WERE TO MAKE LAWS FORBIDDING FOX-HUNTING?

	%
Approve	64
Disapprove	20
Don't know	16

ROWS

It is normal to have rows, although almost a fifth of the population say they don't. But what sparks them off?

Money, or the lack of it, causes more family friction than any other subject, with husbands declaring that wives' spending habits, particularly on clothes, is a source of considerable annoyance.

And if you are in the 25-44 age group and married, you are more likely than most to get steamed up about spending sprees and start shouting matches.

When we have finished arguing about finance, the next point of discord is most likely to centre on the children.

Keeping junior under control can be a stressful experience. Discipline is usually left to Mum. This could account for the fact that twice as many women as men say they have rows about the children. Or perhaps the men are just not listening?

One in ten of us admit to having petty rows about silly issues such as whose turn is it to carry out small jobs around the home. And for married couples in particular, jobs such as failing to wash the dishes or keep the bathroom cabinet tidy, can act as a flashpoint for fury.

Teenagers and young adults are twice as likely than most people to bicker about their social life, while long working hours are a big bone of contention among middle-aged couples.

Some of us seem to like arguing for the sake of arguing. One in 14 Britons say they row about, "nothing in particular"!

Politics in The House of Commons may be at the heart of the argument game, but for the majority of citizens the idea of arguing about politics at home gets a definite thumbs down across most age groups and classes of society.

WHAT WOULD YOU SAY WAS THE WORST DAY OF THE WEEK?

	%
Monday	39
Tuesday	3
Wednesday	4
Thursday	4
Friday	4
Saturday	5
Sunday	12
None	29

DRUGS

A quarter of all 16-24 year olds claim to know where to buy illegal drugs locally which is startling enough to see why two thirds of the nation believes the use of drugs is a very serious problem. Another quarter regard the practice as moderately serious.

Concern about the problem rises still higher among women and the elderly.

And when it comes to heavy drugs such as heroin and cocaine our fears grow greater, with 84 per cent of the population believing them to be a very serious problem.

Lack of discipline in the home and at school is rated by six per cent as the main reason for the increase in drug abuse; while a decline in social standards, not enough control at airports and the ability to make big money are put forward as reasons for the increase.

How many people believe that increased drug use means there has been a fundamental breakdown in British morals?

Four out of ten agree, but over half reject the notion. These views change quite radically depending whether you are young or old. The young are certainly less concerned than average that drugs will bring about a breakdown in society, but the elderly do not share their optimism, and over half of 65 year olds believe illegal drugs have brought about a breakdown of moral standards.

What about the more common drugs? Does the nation think that alcohol abuse is a more serious problem than illegal drugs?

Drugs are definitely more serious say almost six in ten people, with alcohol abuse seen as the most serious problem by a quarter.

Heroin is seen by most people as the most evil menace, with four in ten agreeing it is a problem in their area.

Cocaine is number two, with a fifth of the population expressing concern about its availability and use.

But why does the average person think drug abuse has increased in recent years?

Unemployment, boredom and easier availability through more drug pushers say two thirds.

Who do we think is more responsible for the drug problem in our country today - the person who sells illegal drugs or the person who uses illegal drugs? An overwhelming three-quarters say it is the people who sell the drugs.

What do we think can be done to curb the horror?

Stiffer penalties for persons caught selling drugs say over half the nation. What else? More educational programmes about drug abuse, stiffer penalties for drug users, more treatment programmes, more drug testing at work, and encouraging celebrities to speak out against drugs, say four in ten.

DO YOU HAPPEN TO KNOW OF ANY SPECIFIC PLACE IN THE AREA WHERE YOU LIVE WHERE ILLEGAL DRUGS ARE SOLD, OR KNOW OF ANY PERSON WHO SELLS THEM?

	%
Yes	14
No	83
Not sure	3

WHO DO YOU THINK IS MORE RESPONSIBLE FOR THE DRUG PROBLEM IN OUR COUNTRY TODAY - THE PERSON WHO SELLS ILLEGAL DRUGS OR THE PERSON WHO USES ILLEGAL DRUGS?

	%
Seller	74
User	11
Both	13
No opinion	2

WOULD YOU BE WILLING TO PAY MORE IN TAXES IN ORDER TO FIGHT THE DRUG PROBLEM?

	%
Yes	51
No	39
Depends	5
No opinion	5

MEIN KAMPF
LAHZ

COMMUNICATION

Media

Polls

Books

TV Soaps

MEDIA

Do you believe what you see on television or read in the press?

When asked which medium offers the most truthful source of information, the clear leader was radio, followed by BBC Television. Next came Independent Television.

Bottom of the list came the popular press.

The quality newspapers are top among nationals and rate almost as high as television programmes.

Owners of national newspapers are thought to be very influential as far as Britain's future is concerned.

Margaret Thatcher, her ministers, big business and the City are thought to be most influential but newspaper proprietors are way ahead of the average MP, the Royal Family and the Church.

These are too many newspapers in the hands of too few owners say two-thirds of the nation. The same number feel that newspaper proprietors show too little responsibility for what appears in their papers.

There is too much emphasis on sexy stories by the popular newspapers say four out of five adults, with even more disagreeing that it was all right for newspapers to invade the privacy of ordinary people while gathering a news story. Nine out of ten felt that most newspapers are biased towards one particular political party. Most agree that televising the House of Commons is a good idea but people express concern that MPs will act up to the cameras.

Television does affect our lives 80 per cent of women, for example, believe that TV news stories about violence have made Britons more fearful than they were in the days before there was television.

Twice as many of us believe that TV entertainment shows are worse rather than better compared with five years ago.

Of this group, half believe lower standards are due to poor programme content and bad programming. Too many repeats were blamed by a significant number.

Women are more inclined to agree than men that there is too much sex on TV. The most marked difference in attitudes toward steamy screens is between the young and old. Only a quarter of people between 16 to 34 years old see this as a problem, but four out of five senior citizens do not like so much sex beamed at them.

The young are more likely to be concerned about violence than about sex on TV. The majority of us believe that showing violence is harmful to society but it does not bother us personally. Only half as many men as women are bothered by violence.

HOW WOULD YOU COMPARE TV ENTERTAINMENT THESE DAYS WITH TV ENTERTAINMENT FIVE YEARS AGO. WOULD YOU SAY IT IS BETTER OR WORSE NOW?

	%
Better	27
Worse	56
Don't know	17

WOULD YOU SAY VIOLENCE ON TV BOTHERS YOU OR NOT?

	%
Bothers	37
Does not bother	61
Don't know	2

DO YOU APPROVE OR DISAPPROVE OF THE WAY THE 'POPULAR' NEWSPAPERS HANDLE NEWS OF THE ROYAL FAMILY?

	%
Approve	17
Disapprove	74
Don't know	9

DO YOU THINK THAT THE 'POPULAR NEWSPAPERS TEND TO PLACE TOO MUCH EMPHASIS OR TOO LITTLE EMPHASIS ON 'SEXY' STORIES OR ARE THESE REPORTED AT THE RIGHT LEVEL?

	%
Too much	82
Too little	2
About right	13
Don't know	3

POLLS

Have you ever been interviewed by an opinion pollster? Nearly half the nation has, with almost a fifth having been interviewed at least six times or more.

Where do interviews take place? The street is the most likely venue with nearly three out of four occurring there. Interviews at home are next, with telephone and postal quizzes trailing behind.

Questions about consumer products are by far the most popular polls followed by shops, supermarkets and TV programmes.

How influenced are we by opinion polls? And do we believe their predictions? Nearly half the nation say poll results reflect British public opinion, but women tend to be more sceptical about the results than men. A third disagree, and a quarter of 16 to 24 year olds did not have an opinion either way.

Do people read or listen to the results of polls?

Half the nation say they had noticed the results of a poll or survey during the previous three months. The middle-age groups are most interested. Are your views of interest to anyone else?

Indeed they are.

Government, business and the media are constantly conducting opinion polls to find out what the British public thinks.

Subjects researched vary widely from baked beans to banking from politics to police.

Nine out of ten people think it is pleasant to be asked their opinion. Public opinion polls are popular with two thirds of the nation. They also agree that it is useful and interesting for them to know the opinion of the British in order to make comparisons.

Do people who are interviewed say what they think? Almost two-thirds believe they do.

ON THE SUBJECT OF PUBLIC OPINION IN GENERAL, DO YOU AGREE OR DISAGREE WITH THE STATEMENT, IT IS PLEASANT TO BE ASKED MY OPINION?

	%
Agree	**87**
Disagree	**8**
Don't know	**5**

BOOKS

Who buys what books in Britain? Years ago, when God-fearing citizens arrived home after a hard day at the plough, the only book they were likely to find was...The Bible.

In today's microwave society they are more likely to own a cookery book. Nine out of ten adults claim to own one.

Such is our disaffection with religious matters that the Holy Book now sits at number four.

A dictionary is the second literary priority, with novels slipping in at number three position.

Having satisfied stomach, mind and religious belief, our quest for knowledge moves on to encompass travel - the atlas is number five in the reading register and to be found in a quarter of all British homes.

The perception of life on the other side tends to sharpen views. The older and richer we get, the more likely we are to own a Bible, with almost nine out of ten owning a copy.

Celtic origins also provide a clue about religious beliefs - the Scots and Welsh for example provide Britain's most fruitful Bible-owning belts.

If you are looking for culinary skills then go for the rich man's table every time. The well-off are far more likely than the poor to own a cookery book.

And the rich-poor divide opens up even wider where atlas and encyclopaedia ownership is concerned.

Ownership of basic books is evenly split between men and women with the exception of an atlas. Dreaming of far-away places, or at least wanting to know where they are, is probably more common among men for they are more likely than women to own an atlas.

But how many books does the normal person own and how often do you think people buy books?

The average person owns 197 books and the wealthier you are, the more books you are likely to own. Someone in the well-off bracket is likely to own almost twice the national average.

Conversely, the poor own around half the normal quantity.

Book ownership also varies depending upon where you live. Southerners have an average 237 on their bookshelves, while Scottish bookworms can only muster 124.

The normal person buys on average five books a year, although this rises to eight for the rich, and falls to three for pensioners and the poor. Almost half of all books bought are given away as presents for someone else. The normal person will hand over three a year on average.

But if you have rich relatives living in the south then your chances of receiving a book on your birthday rise significantly - they give away five a year on average.

The overall conclusion is that the more money you have and the better your education, the more likely you are to buy books.

Geographically, the Scots' reputation for careful control of spending is born out by their book purchasing patterns. They buy far less than average and correspondingly give fewer than average as presents.

Affluent Southerners however, buy and therefore own, more books than average.

ROUGHLY HOW MANY BOOKS WOULD YOU SAY YOU HAVE IN YOUR HOME?

	%
None	2
1 - 9	7
10 - 50	25
51 - 100	19
101 - 200	18
201 - 500	17
501 - 1000	5
Over 1000	4
Don't know how many	3

TV SOAPS

Watching soap operas on television is a top priority for millions. In fact it is one of the most normal things to do.

Britain's longest running TV soap "Coronation Street" topped the viewing polls for years before "Eastenders" arrived, but now "Neighbours" is beginning to make an impact.

While the battle for claiming the top viewing figures rages from one soap to another, the nation was asked to name their favourite soap.

"Neighbours" topped the poll with a quarter of the nation's vote. "Coronation Street" came second. "Eastenders" third, "Brookside" fourth with "Dallas" and "Dynasty" filling fifth and sixth places.

What you like has a lot to do with how old you are, your sex and where you live.

The popularity of "Neighbours", relies heavily on the young, with half the under 25's saying it is their favourite compared with 13 per cent of the elderly. The Australian soap wins a third of women's votes compared with 12 per cent of men's and is most popular in Scotland with 40 per cent of the Scots voting it into first place. "Neighbours" is least popular in the South where only 18 per cent vote it their favourite.

Not surprisingly, Northerners give "Coronation Street" a well-above-average vote, but Southerners mark the programme well below the national average.

"Coronation Street" scores badly among the young but is exceedingly popular among the old and less well-off.

"Eastenders" on the other hand, is far more popular in the South than the North or Scotland, and is twice as popular among women as men.

Perhaps it is all something to do with "Dirty Den". The actor in "Eastenders" used to be by far the best-liked character in the TV soaps especially among the 25-34 year olds. He was liked least by the over 65's.

Second in the soap star line-up came Bet Lynch of "Coronation Street". Madge in "Neighbours" and Jack Duckworth of "Coronation Street" tied for third place, with Rita Fairclough of "Coronation Street" taking fifth position in the popularity stakes.

Who don't we like? If you say Mrs Mangel of "Neighbours", you would be quite normal. Over a tenth of the nation singles her out as the person they most dislike among the TV soap stars, with over a fifth of the young confirming this.

Most soap viewers seem to be satisfied with the performance of their idols. Only JR Ewing of "Dallas" fame was the other character named in the unpopularity stakes.

WHAT IS YOUR FAVOURITE TV SOAP OPERA?

	%
Neighbours	23
Coronation Street	13
Eastenders	12
Brookside	6
Dallas	3
Dynasty	9
Other	9
None	34

FAMILY

Homes

Schools

Holidays

Pets

HOMES

If you own your home, or are paying for it with a mortgage, then you are definitely normal. Today, 67 per cent of the nation's dwellings are owner occupied and the younger you are, the more likely you are to own your home.

What sort of home do you live in? Four out of ten of us choose a semi-detached house; a quarter opt for either a detached or terraced house and the remainder set up home in either a flat or bungalow.

How many rooms does a normal home have? Over three quarters have at least five rooms excluding the kitchen and bathroom.

So how does your compare? And how important is it?

When the British public was asked whether their homes were more important than material possessions, 84 per cent said yes. And 92 per cent say they take a great deal of pride in their home and make sure it is well maintained.

Indeed, so house-proud are we, that 62 per cent of us would rather spend money decorating our home than splashing out on a new car.

But why the obsession with owning a home rather than renting? After all, most of our EEC partners prefer to rent and leave the worry of maintenance to a landlord. Research shows that security against eviction is the predominant reason (38 per cent) followed by a desire to leave something for our children (24 per cent) and comfort (21 per cent). Security, independence and a sense of achievement are also powerful reasons and ones that will be immediately recognised by the average home owner.

Is owning your own home the quickest and easiest way to make money? The nation is evenly split in its response, with half believing this and the other half disagreeing. It all depends on whether prices will rise, remain static or even fall. Who can tell?

Who and what is in fashion at home? Technology reigns supreme. Cordless telephones, compact discs, microwave cookers and answering machines are all definitely "in". But if you want to spot the homes that are definitely "out", look for gold bathroom taps, flying ducks on the living room wall and gnomes in the garden.

Do our homes reveal our class?

Gold bathroom taps, jacuzzis and solariums shriek upper class, while the lower classes are more likely to be identified by garden gnomes and DIY work.

The colour and style of your front door offers visitors an insight into your personality.

Although the nation's most popular choice is a varnished wooden front door, one out of six British front doors is painted white making it the most popular colour. In joint second place come red and blue with a tenth of the nation choosing one of these two colours. Green is in fourth position followed by yellow and bottom of the list is black.

WHICH OF THESE BEST DESCRIBES WHERE YOU LIVE?

	%
Semi-detached house	41
Terraced house	25
Detached house	16
Maisonette	3
Farm house or cottage in the country	1
Flat in a block of:	
Up to 10 apartments	5
11 - 50	3
Over 50	1
Other	5

WHICH OF THE FOLLOWING WOULD YOU SAY IS THE MOST IMPORTANT REASON FOR OWNING ONE'S HOME?

	%
Security against eviction	38
Inheritance for children	24
Comfort	21
To make money	6
Don't know/No answer	4
Security for future	3
Some other reason	2
Sense of achievement	1
Independence	1

DO YOU OR YOUR FAMILY OWN YOUR OWN HOME?

	%
Own outright	20
Buying on mortgage	47
Rented from:	
Local Authority	26
Private landlord	6
Hostel, lodging etc	1

SCHOOLS

Who gets the best education in Britain? Are you planning to pay for private education for your children? Which type of school gets the best academic results? These are among the dozens of questions asked by parents and children about their education.

You are normal if you went to a state school or plan to send your children to one. Over six in ten people do so. On average, a tenth of us have paid, or plan to pay, for private education, and if you are in the upper income bracket then the figure rises to one in four.

You are normal if you leave school at 16 - over three-quarters of the nation does. One in ten stays until they are 21 or over.

Do you have a degree? It's unlikely, because only one in ten has. If you are in the upper-income bracket, your chances rise significantly - almost a third of this group holds a degree. Only one per cent of the lower income groups can claim the honour.

What about teaching methods? A third of the nation thinks that the change towards modern methods has gone too far but a fifth say they have not gone far enough.

If you are a parent, are you satisfied with the way in which your children are being educated? Almost three-quarters of us say yes.

The majority believe they are told enough about their childrens' progress, teaching methods and choice of subjects. Three-quarters of parents say teachers seem very pleased when parents go to see them - and three-quarters say it is easy to see teachers. Who runs our schools? Almost seven in ten parents say their children's school organises elections for the job of governors or managers.

What about teenage co-education? Separate the sexes or let them mingle? Over three-quarters believe in the idea of boys and girls over 11 years being taught together.

How far do you travel to school? Nearly 50 per cent are within half a mile of the blackboard and chalk, but one in ten live three miles away. And if you are in the South, you are far more likely to travel greater distances in order to get to school.

DO YOU AGREE OR DISAGREE WITH TEACHERS BEING ALLOWED TO INFLICT CORPORAL PUNISHMENT?

	%
Agree	69
Disagree	27
Don't know	4

SHOULD BOYS AND GIRLS OVER ELEVEN YEARS OF AGE BE TAUGHT SEPARATELY OR SHOULD THEY BE TAUGHT TOGETHER?

	%
Separately	18
Together	77
Don't know	5

SOME PEOPLE SAY THAT SEX EDUCATION OF CHILDREN IS A SUBJECT WHICH SHOULD BE LEFT TO THE PARENTS. OTHERS SAY IT IS A SUBJECT THAT SHOULD BE TAUGHT AT SCHOOL. WHAT DO YOU THINK?

	%
Left to parents	19
Taught at school	33
Both	45
Don't know	3

DO YOU THINK TEACHERS SHOULD OR SHOULD NOT TELL CHILDREN ABOUT HOMOSEXUAL AND LESBIAN PRACTICES?

	%
Should	50
Should not	42
Don't know	8

THINKING BACK OVER THE LAST FEW YEARS, DO YOU THINK THE GENERAL STANDARD OF EDUCATION AT YOUR CHILD'S SCHOOL HAS GONE UP, GONE DOWN, OR REMAINED ABOUT THE SAME?

	%
Gone up	16
Gone down	26
Same	47
Don't know	11

HOLIDAYS

Where are you most likely to go for your annual summer holiday? Answer: generally abroad and more specifically, Spain. A third of us choose Spain, making it by far the most popular destination, followed by France and then Greece. So if you are sitting on a charter flight on your way to the Costas, relax, you're normal!

The majority of us, nearly eight in ten, have been abroad. Interestingly, men are more likely to have been to a foreign country than women, probably because of military service and the greater likelihood of business trips.

Most Britons have also been to the UK seaside, but if you have never seen the sea then you are one in 50.

Having decided to leave Blighty behind for a spell, most of us like a quick getaway.

Almost three quarters take off in a plane whilst the rest go by sea. The dominance of air travel is presumably due to the growth of low-cost package holidays and the determination to get the suntan-oil rubbed in as quickly as possible. The lower your income, the more likely you are to travel by plane.

If however, you are in a higher income group, then you are more likely to take your car across the Channel.

When British holidaymakers arrive abroad, over half stay in hotels, a quarter cater for themselves in tents, caravans, villas or apartments and the rest move in with relatives or friends.

Most people deliberately put aside money for the all-important overseas break. Six in ten holidaymakers save up specially while a further three in ten dip into existing savings.

One in ten of us buys the holiday with a credit card and one in 50 gets their bank to lend them the money.

Once abroad, two-thirds of British look after their own spending money but when one partner holds the purse strings, it tends to be the man.

Security is a high priority for most and almost seven in ten take travellers cheques.

Three-quarters of holiday meals are paid for in local currency, but a credit card is the most likely standby if the holiday money runs out.

Are we satisfied with our foreign holidays?

Nine in ten say yes.

What do we want once we are abroad? If you go for sunshine then join the club, it's our top priority. A busy nightlife is important for young adults whilst the over 65's regard re-uniting with friends and relatives as a priority.

All the effort and money that goes into producing the glossy holiday brochures appears to be worthwhile. For four in ten adults choose a holiday after leafing through the booklets.

Only five per cent are tempted by special offers from travel agents or tour operators and a similarly small fraction are won over by advertising.

Travellers put far more reliance on what is said by friends or relatives when deciding where to go, with a quarter of the nation heeding such advice.

When it comes to booking a foreign holiday, we prefer to put our faith in travel agents. Almost seven in ten holidays abroad are arranged through an agent.

And although we may be keen on globe-trotting the chance to travel in space gets the thumbs down. Six out of ten reject the idea of a trip in space. Except of course, if you happen to be young. Almost six out of ten young people are likely to say yes.

WHAT DO YOU WANT OUT OF A HOLIDAY ABROAD?

Sunshine/good weather	61
Change of scenery/getting away from it all	17
Rest/relaxation	31
See how others live/learn other languages/meet other nationalities	16
Nightlife/activities	17
Good food/drink etc/hotel/ accommodation/amenities	20
Good beaches/sea	5
Good scenery/countryside/ sightseeing	16
Value for money/inexpensive holiday	6
Visiting friends/relatives	5
Other	5

PETS

Dogs are the most popular pet in Britain with almost one in three householders owning one. Second are cats, with a quarter of us enjoying the fur and purr while one in ten go for pet fish. Budgies, canaries and rabbits are less popular, with each creature being owned by five per cent of homes.

There are more cats than dogs, as most dog owners tend to have only one, whereas a quarter of feline fans own two, and one in nine own three or more.

Who among us is most likely to own a dog? It is the young adults who presumably like to see their children race around with Rover or alternatively use faithful Fido as a substitute for human friendship? Interestingly, if you happen to be in this group you are less likely than average to own a rabbit which must come as something of a relief, particularly for the rabbit.

The elderly however, are least likely to own a dog with only one in ten householders having one, which seems to suggest that once children have grown up and left the nest, then a dog's days are numbered.

Dogs are liked equally by the rich and poor but the rich own more cats than the poor, who are more likely to own a budgie.

Neither do our senior citizens keep up with the cat average. Kitty is only likely to be found in one out of ten elderly households.

Cats are more likely to be found in castles rather than council houses but when it comes to the shrill trills of a pet budgie, the situation is reversed.

Where in Britain are you least likely to find a cat? Try Scottish homes with almost half the national average in cat ownership, which is probably just as well, because the Scots have twice as many budgies and canaries as normal.

Is it normal to own both a cat and a dog? The chances are that one in three cat owners will also have a dog, whereas under one in three dog owners is likely to have a cat, if you see what we mean.

Do you think your pet understands what you say to it? The majority of pet owners - four out of five do, even those whose pet happens to be swimming around in a goldfish bowl!

And the older you become, the more likely you are to have a rapport with your animal, fish or bird.

Almost all over 65's are convinced their pets understand them, whereas only three quarters of the under 25's believe they do.

Good advice to any pet who doesn't have a good natter to his or her owner, is to move to the North where nine out of ten people believe their pets understand them - 10 per cent higher than the rest of Britain.

Men and women differ very little in their attitude towards pets except canaries and budgies. Among those senior citizens who own a caged-bird, women almost invariably will have only one, but more than a third of the men in this group have two or more.

If you own a cat then your second pet will probably be a rabbit. Dog owners tend to choose a fish as their second pet.

WHICH, IF ANY, OF THE FOLLOWING PETS DO YOU HAVE IN YOUR HOME?

Cat	24
Dog	30
Budgie, Canary	5
Rabbit	5
Fish	10
Other	7
None	45

DO YOU THINK THAT YOUR PET EVER UNDERSTANDS WHAT YOU SAY TO IT?

	%
Yes	81
No	16
Don't know	3

WHAT IS 'IN' AND 'OUT'?

The facts and figures so far have been selected from Gallup Poll's data bank and other authoritative sources. Every week Gallup Poll ask members of the public what they think is "in" or "out" of fashion.

We have selected some of this information and devised ten quizzes so that you can test yourself against what the nation thinks.

TEST YOURSELF

People often say that things are 'in' or 'out'. Test yourself against what the nation thinks.

Put a number between 1 and 10 in each of the boxes below. The more you think something is 'in' then the higher mark you give it.

For example, if you think Godparents are very much in fashion then you might put a figure 8 in the box opposite. Alternatively if you think they are totally out of fashion, then only give them a score of 1 or 2.

Princess Di look	☐
Belief in flying saucers	☐
Belief in ghosts	☐
Belief in God	☐
Godparents	☐
Christmas stockings	☐
Going to the pantomime	☐
Traditional Christmas Dinner	☐
New Year's Resolutions	☐
Reading Sci-Fi novels	☐

Now turn the page to see how you compare with the rest of the nation.

TEST YOURSELF

How the nation scores

Princess Di look	4
Belief in flying saucers	2
Belief in ghosts	3
Belief in God	4
Godparents	5
Christmas stockings	5
Going to the pantomime	6
Traditional Christmas Dinner	9
New Year's Resolutions	5
Reading Sci-Fi novels	4

TEST YOURSELF

ROMANCE

Kissing under mistletoe	☐
Kissing hands	☐
Chastity	☐
Nude beaches	☐
Traditional weddings	☐
Love letters	☐
Women proposing	☐
Computer dating	☐
Getting engaged	☐
Wearing wedding rings	☐

TEST YOURSELF

How the nation scores

Kissing under mistletoe	6
Kissing hands	1
Chastity	3
Nude beaches	5
Traditional weddings	8
Love letters	2
Women proposing	5
Computer dating	6
Getting engaged	6
Wearing wedding rings	8

TEST YOURSELF

FINANCE

Shopping at Marks & Spencer	☐
Saving	☐
Giving to charities	☐
Buying Japanese goods	☐
Buying through mail order	☐
Starting own business	☐
Answer-phones	☐
Porsche cars	☐
Car telephones	☐
Furry dice in cars	☐

TEST YOURSELF

How the nation scores

Shopping at Marks & Spencer	7
Saving	7
Giving to charities	9
Buying Japanese goods	6
Buying through mail order	7
Starting own business	9
Answer phones	7
Porsche cars	7
Car telephones	8
Furry dice in cars	2

TEST YOURSELF

LEISURE

- Plastic flowers ☐
- Garden gnomes ☐
- Yoga ☐
- Playing Cards ☐
- Breakfast in bed ☐
- Sherry ☐
- Herbal tea ☐
- Real fur coats ☐
- Pyjamas ☐
- Hats for men ☐

TEST YOURSELF

How the nation scores

Plastic flowers	2
Garden gnomes	2
Yoga	4
Playing Cards	4
Breakfast in bed	2
Sherry	3
Herbal tea	4
Real fur coats	1
Pyjamas	3
Hats for men	1

TEST YOURSELF

LIFE

Smoking cigarettes	☐
Paying for private medical care	☐
Contact lenses	☐
Acupuncture	☐
Tidiness	☐
Politeness	☐
Toothpicks	☐
Fatter people	☐
Thinner people	☐
Aerobics	☐

TEST YOURSELF

How the nation scores

Smoking cigarettes	2
Paying for private medical care	8
Contact lenses	7
Acupuncture	6
Tidiness	4
Politeness	4
Toothpicks	2
Fatter people	4
Thinner people	7
Aerobics	6

TEST YOURSELF

LUCK

- Horoscopes ☐
- Belief in Black Magic ☐
- Singing Telegrams ☐
- Singing in the bath ☐
- Tolerance of other people ☐
- Enjoyment of art ☐
- Sending 'Thank You' cards ☐
- Bingo ☐
- Betting ☐
- Fruit machines ☐

TEST YOURSELF

How the nation scores

Horoscopes	6
Belief in Black Magic	2
Singing Telegrams	3
Singing in the bath	4
Tolerance of other people	3
Enjoyment of art	7
Sending 'Thank You' cards	6
Bingo	5
Betting	6
Fruit machines	4

TEST YOURSELF

PEOPLE

Friendly neighbours	☐
Speaking a foreign language	☐
The Common Market	☐
Women with pierced ears	☐
Housewarming parties	☐
Sending flowers	☐
Bikinis	☐
Films by Charlie Chaplin	☐
Teddy Bears	☐
Single parent families	☐

TEST YOURSELF

How the nation scores

Friendly neighbours	6
Speaking a foreign language	6
The Common Market	4
Women with pierced ears	8
Housewarming parties	4
Sending flowers	8
Bikini's	5
Films by Charlie Chaplin	3
Teddy Bears	7
Single parent families	7

TEST YOURSELF

AGGRESSION

- Learning Self Defence ☐
- Respect for authority ☐
- Wearing medals ☐
- Playing squash ☐
- Gazumping ☐
- Honest policeman ☐
- Films by Clint Eastwood ☐
- Swearing ☐
- Working hard ☐
- Skateboards ☐

TEST YOURSELF

How the nation scores

Learning Self Defence	8
Respect for authority	2
Wearing medals	2
Playing squash	7
Gazumping	5
Honest policeman	5
Films by Clint Eastwood	5
Swearing	7
Working hard	6
Skateboards	6

TEST YOURSELF

COMMUNICATION

The Sun	☐
The Times	☐
Going to cinema	☐
Satellite TV	☐
Watching videos	☐
Cable TV	☐
Going to the theatre	☐
Going to libraries	☐
Children's comics	☐
"Neighbours"	☐

TEST YOURSELF

How the nation scores

The Sun	5
The Times	4
Going to cinema	4
Satellite TV	7
Watching videos	9
Cable TV	5
Going to the theatre	6
Going to Libraries	5
Children's Comics	5
Neighbours	8

TEST YOURSELF

FAMILY

Home computers ☐
Microwaves ☐
Double glazing ☐
Dishwashers ☐
D.I.Y. ☐
Keeping animals in zoos ☐
Sending children to private schools ☐
Holidays in Spain ☐
Skiing holidays ☐
Self-catering holidays ☐

TEST YOURSELF

How the nation scores

Home computers	8
Microwaves	9
Double glazing	8
Dishwashers	7
D.I.Y.	9
Keeping animals in zoos	3
Sending children to private schools	6
Holidays in Spain	7
Skiing holidays	8
Self-catering holidays	7

? ARE YOU NORMAL

PRESENTS AND CARDS BY POST

T-SHIRTS
? "Are You Normal" cotton T-Shirts have the question boldly printed on the front, with results from one of Gallup's questions on the back.

Surprise your friends by wearing one or give one as a present.

Choose your own subject from Rude Habits, Pets, Bed, Christmas or Romance.

GREETING CARDS
Cards with a difference for birthdays or special occasions. Your family or friends will enjoy one of these new card ideas. Complete with envelopes, there are four cards in a pack. Each contains the different results of a nationwide quiz on Bed, Rude Habits, Romance and Pets.

BOOKS
If you have enjoyed this book and would like a friend or relative to receive a copy, then order it by post. Should you want it delivered straight to them then please fill in their name and address on a separate piece of paper and write BOOK DELIVERY at the top.

? ARE YOU NORMAL

ORDER FORM

All prices include postage and packing. Delivery is normally within 28 days.

Please list the items you want. Enter the amount in the column on the right. Total the column at the bottom and complete the form with your name and address.

T-SHIRT £7.50 each. Choose your subject and enter quantity in box.

	Small	Medium	Large	
Rude Habits				
Pets				
Bed				Amount
Romance				£ . . . .

GREETING CARDS Pack of four £3.20
Please send (quantity) . . . . . pack/s Amount £ . . . .

BOOK for £4.60 including postage and packing
Please send (quantity) . . . . . copy/s Amount £ . . . .

Total Amount £ . . . .

Cut out page and send to Dept. RUN Vine House Publications, Waldenbury, North Common, Chailey, East Sussex. BN8 4DR
I enclose a cheque/postal order no. . . . . made payable to VINE HOUSE PUBLICATIONS

or please charge £ . . . . to my Access/ Mastercard or Visa

card no ☐☐☐☐☐☐☐☐☐☐☐☐☐☐☐☐

Name . . . .

Address . . . .

. . . .

Town . . . . Post Code . . . .

Signature . . . .